OLWEUS®

BULLYING PREVENTION PROGRAM

SCHOOLWIDE GUIDE

Dan Olweus, Ph.D., and Susan P. Limber, Ph.D.

Vicki Crocker Flerx, Ph.D.

Nancy Mullin, M.Ed.

Jane Riese, L.S.W.

Marlene Snyder, Ph.D.

HAZELDEN

naespfoundation
ENDOWING LEADERSHIP AND LEARNING

Hazelden
Center City, MN 55012-0176

1-800-328-9000
1-651-213-4590 (Fax)
www.hazelden.org

This Schoolwide Guide and the accompanying Teacher Guide are revised and partly expanded versions of *Olweus' Core Program Against Bullying and Antisocial Behavior: A Teacher Handbook* by Dan Olweus (privately printed, 2006). Distributed by Hazelden.

ISBN: 978-1-59285-374-8

Cover design by David Spohn
Cover photo by Tad Saddoris
Interior design and typesetting by Kinne Design

What Is the Purpose of This Schoolwide Guide?

The purpose of this Schoolwide Guide is to provide step-by-step instructions on how to implement the *Olweus® Bullying Prevention Program* in an entire school setting. The Schoolwide Guide is used mainly by school leadership or a school's Bullying Prevention Coordinating Committee, or BPCC for short (the team established to guide schoolwide implementation).

It is important that you read through the Schoolwide Guide in its entirety before beginning implementation. Throughout this guide, you will see:

RESEARCH FACTS

> These facts highlight some of the important research findings that Dr. Dan Olweus, his collaborators, and other researchers have learned over more than thirty-five years of studying bullying.

IMPLEMENTATION TIPS

> These tips and strategies, gleaned from others' experiences, will make program implementation easier for you.

How to Use the DVD and the CD-ROM

This Schoolwide Guide comes with a DVD and a CD-ROM. Here's how to use these components.

Accessing the DVD Video Resources

The DVD is divided into two parts:

Part 1: Program Overview

Part 1 gives an overview of why it is important to address bullying and what the *Olweus Bullying Prevention Program* is.

Part 2: Program Components

Part 2 gives a more in-depth overview of the *Olweus Bullying Prevention Program* components at the schoolwide, classroom, individual, and community levels.

Whenever you see this icon in this guide, you are encouraged to view the DVD. To access Part 1 and Part 2 on the DVD, put the disk in a DVD player. A menu will automatically appear on your screen. Select the title and push Play. You can pause the video at any time while it is playing.

Accessing the CD-ROM Print Resources

The CD-ROM contains print resources, such as the handouts and templates mentioned in this guide. All of these resources are in either PDF format (which can be accessed using Adobe Reader) or in Microsoft Word. If you do not have Adobe Reader, you can download it for free at www.adobe.com.

Whenever you see this icon in this guide, there is a copy of this resource on the CD-ROM. The number on the icon corresponds to the number of the document on the CD-ROM. An SP symbol (SP) near the icon indicates the document is also available in Spanish.

To access the documents on the CD-ROM, put the disk in your computer's CD-ROM player. Open your version of Adobe Reader or Microsoft Word, and then open the documents by finding them on your CD-ROM drive. The PDF documents cannot be modified, but they can be printed for use in individual school settings without concern for copyright infringement. For a list of what is contained on the CD-ROM, see the Read Me First document on the CD-ROM.

• • •

Endorsements for the *Olweus Bullying Prevention Program*

"Dr. Dan Olweus and his team have gone from strength to strength in their bullying prevention efforts with this new guide. I concur with the authors' stress on systems change as the key to violence prevention, and in expanding the audience outside the doors of the school to members of the community. Beautifully written and carefully researched, this guide comes highly recommended."

John H. Hoover
Interim Associate Dean, College of Education
St. Cloud State University, St. Cloud, Minnesota
author of *The Bullying Prevention Handbook*

"The *Olweus Bullying Prevention Program* has had a positive impact on our entire school of over 650 students and staff. We have become a safe, predictable environment for all, and all feel empowered to make a difference. Following our first full year of implementation, the reported bullying referrals have decreased by 68 percent."

Rebecca Dahl, Principal
and Casey Bertram, Assistant Principal
Edgerton Elementary School, Kalispell, Montana

"Philadelphia is the seventh largest school district in the United States. Since 2001, the *Olweus Bullying Prevention Program* has been implemented in 40 schools and our data shows that when implemented with fidelity, the program not only reduces bullying behaviors, but it effectively provides the framework for systemic improvement in school climate and safety."

Vernard Trent
Director of the Office of School Climate and Safety
School District of Philadelphia, Pennsylvania

Contents

CONTINUED ON NEXT PAGE

• • •

Acknowledgments

Because the *Olweus Bullying Prevention Program* has had a long history (over thirty-five years) and has been implemented by so many around the world, it is impossible to properly acknowledge all who have contributed to its development and success. However, we want to highlight a few who have played particularly critical roles.

First, we wish to thank the many educators, students, parents, and community members who have helped to implement the program in schools worldwide and from whom we have learned so much.

We also wish to thank the many certified Olweus trainers, who, on a daily basis, work hard to help schools be successful in their implementation of the program and who seem to have a never-ending supply of energy and new ideas.

Thanks to Del Elliott and Sharon Mihalic with the Center for the Study and Prevention of Violence at the University of Colorado at Boulder for being early supporters of the program in the United States and for helping to get the word out about the *Olweus Bullying Prevention Program* through the Blueprints project.

We wish to thank the Office of Juvenile Justice and Delinquency Prevention (OJJDP) for funding the first implementation and evaluation of the program in the United States.

We wish to also acknowledge the work of those South Carolina schools that participated in the original implementation of the program in the United States.

Thanks also to those involved in the early statewide efforts in Massachusetts and Pennsylvania. Their experiences resulted in the development of many practical tools for schools, some of which are included in this guide.

Special thanks to Celia Arriaga, of the Seattle Public Schools, for her dedication in developing the Spanish translations.

We appreciate and acknowledge our many friends and colleagues at Hazelden, particularly Kris Van Hoof-Haines and Sue Thomas, who are our valued collaborators. We also thank Bonnie Dudovitz, who helped develop this guide.

And finally, we wish to thank the many schools that have submitted samples of implementation strategies for this Schoolwide Guide.

• • •

Introduction

Welcome to the *Olweus Bullying Prevention Program,* or *OBPP* for short. *OBPP* is the most researched and best-known bullying prevention program available today. Developed by Dr. Dan Olweus of Norway, one of the authors of this guide, *OBPP* has over thirty-five years of research behind it and has been implemented throughout the world, in countries such as the United States, Canada, England, Mexico, Iceland, Germany, Sweden, and Croatia, in addition to Norway.

Olweus is pronounced Ol-VAY-us.

OBPP is recognized by the Center for the Study and Prevention of Violence as one of only eleven (at the time of publication) Blueprints Model Programs and by the Substance Abuse and Mental Health Services Administration (SAMHSA) as a Model Program—two of the highest honors a prevention program can attain. It has also received numerous awards from other organizations dedicated to addressing the issue of bullying and violence among students.

As someone who works with young people, you know that even with your best efforts, a student may still experience bullying in classrooms, school hallways, the lunchroom, and the playground or athletic fields. And bullying isn't limited to the school grounds; it exists at school bus stops, community parks, summer camps, neighborhoods, homes, cyberspace, and anywhere that young people gather.

To stop bullying, it needs to be addressed at all levels of a student's experience. Unlike a curriculum that only addresses bullying at the classroom level and for a limited period of time, *OBPP* addresses bullying at the schoolwide, classroom, individual, and community levels.

Accordingly, students receive a consistent, reinforced message about bullying over an extended period of time and in a variety of settings. Because bullying has such wide-ranging effects, *OBPP* is designed for all students, not just those who are bullied or those who bully others.

The goal of *OBPP* is to change the norms around bullying behavior and to restructure the school setting itself so that bullying is less likely to occur or be rewarded. The implementation of *OBPP* needs to be seen as a long-term effort—not something that is "completed" in a year.

Also because of its comprehensive approach, it is a great advantage if *OBPP* is implemented across all grade levels in a school building at approximately the same time. Although *OBPP* takes a concerted and coordinated effort to implement, it has been proven in a number of scientific evaluations to reduce the occurrence of bullying problems and improve the school environment.

What Is Bullying?

In order to address the issue of bullying, it is important to clearly understand how bullying is defined. Here is a commonly used definition:

> A person is bullied when he or she is exposed, repeatedly and over time, to negative actions on the part of one or more other persons, and he or she has difficulty defending himself or herself.[1]

Expressed in more everyday language, one might say: Bullying is when someone repeatedly and on purpose says or does mean or hurtful things to another person who has a hard time defending himself or herself.

The definition of bullying has three major components: First, it is aggressive behavior that involves unwanted, negative actions. Second, bullying typically involves a pattern of behavior repeated over time. Finally, it involves an imbalance of power or strength.

Bullying can take many forms, such as physical hitting, verbal taunts, spreading of false rumors, intentional social exclusion, and sending nasty messages on a cell phone or over the Internet.

Note: Throughout this guide we have been careful to avoid using the terms "bully" and "victim" as much as possible when describing students who bully others or who are bullied by others. This is intentional, and we encourage you to avoid these labels as well when talking with your students. However, you may notice that such terms are often used in research literature as a convenient way to describe bullying situations. In a few places in this guide where we are talking about the research, we will occasionally use these terms to facilitate the reading of the text.

Bullying is when someone says or does mean things to another student.

— KINDERGARTEN STUDENT

Why Is It Important to Address Bullying in Schools?

Here are some stories about bullying.

MICHAEL'S STORY

Michael, age ten, was bullied at school nearly every day. Boys punched and kicked him on the playground (just out of sight from the teachers), stole his lunch money, and called him nasty names. Michael complained to his parents and the school nurse about stomach pains and headaches and often stayed home from school, but for months he said nothing about the bullying.

When Michael's schoolwork began to suffer, his teacher asked for a meeting with Michael and his parents. At the meeting, they pressed him about why he was having trouble in school, and he finally admitted that he was being "picked on" by a few boys in his class. When asked why he hadn't told anyone sooner, he responded, "It wouldn't have done any good. I guess this is just how fourth grade is going to be."

KATIE'S STORY

Katie, an eighth-grade student with cerebral palsy, was repeatedly bullied by a male classmate. The boy called her names, such as "retard" and "stupid," blocked her path down the hall, and even rammed her wheelchair into walls. After three years of abuse, Katie and her parents successfully sued the school district. A lawsuit against the boy's family was settled out of court.

JENNY'S STORY

Jenny, a new kindergarten student, had been looking forward to riding the school bus all summer, so her mother was puzzled when, after only a week, Jenny asked if her mom could drop her off at school instead. When her mother asked why she didn't want to ride the bus anymore, Jenny admitted that some of the third- and fourth-grade girls on the bus had been taking her lunch each morning and calling her "baby."

For Students and Their Futures

Every day, there are many students, like these, who come to school terrified that they will be bullied yet again. Students who are bullied may become depressed and develop low self-esteem. Many of them develop health problems such as stomachaches and headaches, and their schoolwork is likely to suffer. Some bullied students may have suicidal thoughts and may even end their own lives. The effects on students who are bullied can last far into the future, long after they are out of school. It is an obvious human right for every student to feel safe in school and to be spared the repeated degradation and humiliation that come from being bullied.

Students who bully others also have problems but typically of a very different nature. Many bullying students tend to engage in other "antisocial" behaviors such as breaking rules, shoplifting and vandalizing property, drinking alcohol and smoking at a relatively young age, and carrying a weapon. There are also clear indications that bullying students, in particular boys, are at a greater risk of continuing on an antisocial path involving crime and substance abuse in young adulthood. These facts make it clear that preventing bullying is important also for the sake of students who bully others.

And bystanders who witness bullying are affected as well. They often feel afraid at school, powerless to change the situation, and perhaps guilty for not taking action. Or they may be drawn into the bullying themselves and feel bad about it afterward. All of this may gradually change the group or classroom attitudes and norms in a harsher, less empathetic direction.

For a Healthy School Climate

When a school allows bullying to continue, the entire school climate is affected. The environment can become one of fear and disrespect, hampering the ability of students to learn. Students may feel insecure and tend not to like school very well. When students don't see the adults at school acting to prevent or intervene in bullying situations, they may feel that teachers and other school staff have little control over the students and don't care what happens to them.

As a staff we can do lots of things that will make a difference, but we are kidding ourselves if we think we're going to build positive student belonging without addressing our school's peer culture and how kids treat one another. The *Olweus Bullying Prevention Program* has helped to make positive student belonging a real possibility.

— A MIDDLE SCHOOL PRINCIPAL

I really think our school's bullying prevention program has stopped the ugly bullying. I used to get glares from some kids and they wouldn't let me play with them. I'm glad that's changed!

— AN ELEMENTARY STUDENT

For the Larger Community

The effects of bullying are so devastating and profound that over the last few years at least thirty (at the time of publication) state laws against bullying have been adopted. In addition to a general concern for student safety and well-being, some of the motivation for passing these laws includes the perception that a number of school shootings have been carried out by students who felt bullied, excluded, or threatened by their peers. The effects of these violent incidents on students, families, schools, and entire communities are felt long after the traumatic events occurred. The community as a whole benefits when students like school and have a variety of community settings where they feel they belong.

For the Purposes of Risk Management for Schools

There have also been civil suits brought against schools and school systems over bullying incidents, some with damages in the millions of dollars. It is important to realize that, like sexual harassment and racial discrimination, some forms of bullying are illegal actions and must be treated as such.

It Is a Smart Investment

The cost of implementing a research-based bullying prevention program with documented effects is small compared to the potential societal benefits. *OBPP* materials cost only $1,500 to $3,200 for an individual school (with additional funding needed for administering the schoolwide questionnaire, staff training, and program administration), while one recent study showed that "each high-risk juvenile who is prevented from adopting a life of crime could save the country between $1.7 million and $2.3 million." [2]

This Schoolwide Guide will give you the information you need to effectively implement the *Olweus Bullying Prevention Program* in your entire school setting. Making this program a schoolwide effort, including teachers' actions and initiatives in their classrooms, can have a profound impact on one of the most difficult issues students face today—bullying.

Stop

Before moving on to the next chapter, please take a few minutes to read the Recognizing the Many Faces of Bullying document on the Schoolwide Guide CD-ROM. This article provides an in-depth discussion of what bullying is, the type of students who bully others and are bullied, the short- and long-term consequences of bullying, and why bullying happens.

If you have a copy of the *OBPP* Teacher Guide, please also watch the bullying scenarios provided on the Teacher Guide DVD. These scenarios will give you a better sense of the emotional impact of bullying.

You may also want to read about two specific bullying issues—cyber-bullying and bullying of students based on sexual orientation. There are articles on both of these topics on the Schoolwide Guide CD-ROM.

• • •

The biggest change with our students after going through the *Olweus Bullying Prevention Program* is they now know how to care for one another.

— AN ELEMENTARY SCHOOL COUNSELOR

You know, we kids can work on this, but it takes teachers that really care.

— AN ELEMENTARY STUDENT

1

Introducing the *Olweus Bullying Prevention Program*

WHAT YOU WILL LEARN IN CHAPTER 1	
	• the components of *OBPP* • the history and research behind the program • what resources are available to help you in its implementation

What Is the *Olweus Bullying Prevention Program?*

As stated earlier, the *Olweus Bullying Prevention Program (OBPP)* is the most researched and best-known bullying prevention program available today. With over thirty-five years of research and successful implementation all over the world, *OBPP* is a whole-school program that has been proven to prevent or reduce bullying throughout a school setting.

OBPP is used at the school, classroom, and individual levels and includes methods to reach out to parents and the community for involvement and support. School administrators, teachers, and other staff are primarily responsible for introducing and implementing the program. These efforts are designed to improve peer relations and make the school a safer and more positive place for students to learn and develop.

What Are the Goals of *OBPP?*

The goals of the program are

- to reduce existing bullying problems among students
- to prevent the development of new bullying problems
- to achieve better peer relations at school

For Whom Is *OBPP* Designed?

OBPP is designed for students in elementary, middle, and junior high schools (students age five to fifteen years old). All students participate in most aspects of the program, while students identified as bullying others, or as targets of bullying, receive additional individualized interventions.

With adaptation the program can also be used in high schools, although research has not measured the program's effectiveness beyond tenth grade. In addition, classroom support materials are not currently available for high school students. Chapter 17 of this guide talks about adapting the program for use in a high school setting.

Because *OBPP* is not a curriculum, its core principles, rules, and supportive materials could be adapted for use by any program that children and youth attend on a regular basis, such as after-school programs, camps, or community youth programs. The core principles and rules could be integrated into these existing programs' policies and routines. With appropriate staff training, these non-school programs can be effective in preventing bullying and helping students understand that bullying is not just a school issue, but one that spills over into all areas of their lives.

What Are the *OBPP* Materials?

Schoolwide Guide

This Schoolwide Guide, with accompanying DVD and CD-ROM, provides step-by-step instructions on how to implement the program in the entire school setting. The Schoolwide Guide is used mainly by your school's Bullying Prevention Coordinating Committee (BPCC), the group that is established to guide schoolwide implementation.

Ideally, every person in leadership at your school and all members of your BPCC should have a copy of this guide. (If at any time you need to reorder this

The power of the *Olweus Bullying Prevention Program* lies in staff and students using common language to address bullying situations. A message is carried out to students saying bullying will not be tolerated here.

— A JUNIOR HIGH SCHOOL COUNSELOR

Schoolwide Guide or any other *OBPP* materials, contact Hazelden Publishing at 1-800-328-9000 or 1-651-213-4000.)

Teacher Guide

The Teacher Guide, with accompanying DVD and CD-ROM, serves as the primary program implementation tool for teachers and other classroom support staff. It highlights the important role teachers play both in the classroom and in schoolwide efforts in preventing and addressing bullying. All the resources teachers need to implement the program, except for the Olweus Bullying Questionnaire, are provided in the guide or on the accompanying DVD and CD-ROM.

Ideally, every teacher should have a copy of the Teacher Guide. If this is not possible, we recommend that each Teacher Guide be shared among no more than three teachers.

Your school leadership and each member of your BPCC will also need to have a copy of the Teacher Guide, because it includes much more in-depth information about bullying and the various components of *OBPP*.

Olweus Bullying Questionnaire

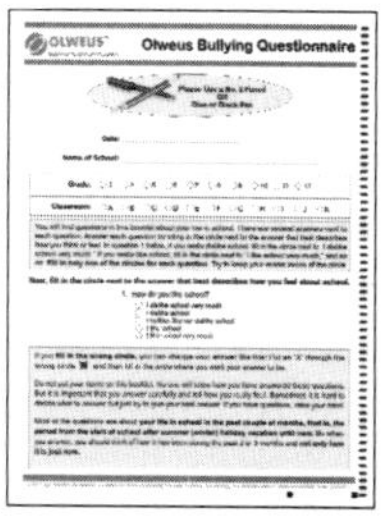

The Olweus Bullying Questionnaire is administered to all students in grades 3–12 before the program begins and at regular intervals (ideally each year) from then on. School leadership and members of the BPCC oversee the implementation of this questionnaire. More information about the questionnaire is provided in chapter 5.

What Are the Components of the Program?

OBPP is not a classroom curriculum. It is a whole-school, systems-change program at four different levels. In the table on the next page are the program components for each of these levels. Each component is discussed in more detail in later chapters.

I think schools really find the *Olweus Bullying Prevention Program* attractive because it's schoolwide. It involves all school staff, students, and even parents in bullying prevention.

— PREVENTION SPECIALIST

GENERAL REQUIREMENTS

Generate awareness and involvement on the part of the adults in the school.

SCHOOL-LEVEL COMPONENTS

- Establish a Bullying Prevention Coordinating Committee.
- Conduct committee and staff trainings.
- Administer the Olweus Bullying Questionnaire schoolwide.
- Hold staff discussion group meetings.
- Introduce the school rules against bullying.
- Review and refine the school's supervisory system.
- Hold a school kick-off event to launch the program.
- Involve parents.

CLASSROOM-LEVEL COMPONENTS

- Post and enforce schoolwide rules against bullying.
- Hold regular class meetings.
- Hold meetings with students' parents.

INDIVIDUAL-LEVEL COMPONENTS

- Supervise students' activities.
- Ensure that all staff intervene on the spot when bullying occurs.
- Hold meetings with students involved in bullying.
- Hold meetings with parents of involved students.
- Develop individual intervention plans for involved students.

COMMUNITY-LEVEL COMPONENTS

- Involve community members on the Bullying Prevention Coordinating Committee.
- Develop partnerships with community members to support your school's program.
- Help to spread anti-bullying messages and principles of best practice in the community.

What Are the Effects of the *Olweus Bullying Prevention Program?*

OBPP has been more thoroughly evaluated than any other bullying prevention/reduction program so far. Six large-scale evaluations, involving more than 40,000 students, have documented results such as the following:[1]

- Average reductions by 20 to 70 percent in student reports of being bullied and bullying others. Peer and teacher ratings of bullying problems have yielded roughly similar results.
- Marked reductions in student reports of general antisocial behavior, such as vandalism, fighting, theft, and truancy.
- Clear improvements in the classroom social climate, as reflected in students' reports of improved order and discipline, more positive social relationships, and more positive attitudes toward schoolwork and school.

For students in grades 4–7, most of these positive results can be seen after only eight months of intervention work, given reasonably good implementation of the program. For students in grades 8–10, it may take somewhat more time, maybe two years, to achieve equally good results.

The program design has also been influenced by detailed *OBPP* research on how teacher and school factors affect implementation of the program. Interested readers are referred to the article "Predicting Teachers' and Schools' Implementation of the Olweus Bullying Prevention Program: A Multilevel Study" by Jan Helge Kallestad and Dan Olweus.[2]

Using *OBPP* will also help you meet portions of many federal mandates or programs you are probably already administering, such as Safe and Drug Free Schools, school connectedness, high-stakes testing, juvenile delinquency prevention, school drop-out prevention, school health programs, suicide prevention, and the promotion of developmental assets.

New research has also shown a positive link between bullying and student achievement. Preventing bullying may help your school make improvements in statewide student achievement assessments/No Child Left Behind requirements as well.[3]

What Is the History behind the *Olweus Bullying Prevention Program?*

Although bullying problems among students have been around for centuries, it wasn't until the early 1970s that Dr. Dan Olweus initiated the first systematic research study in the world on these problems. The results were published in a Swedish book in 1973 and in the United States in 1978 under the title *Aggression in the Schools: Bullies and Whipping Boys*. For a considerable period of time, up to the early 1990s, there was very little attention to and research on the topic of bullying outside of Scandinavia.

In 1983, after three adolescent boys in northern Norway committed suicide, most likely as a consequence of severe bullying by peers, the country's Ministry of Education initiated a national campaign against bullying in schools. In that context, the first version of what has later become known as the *Olweus Bullying Prevention Program* was developed.

The program was carefully evaluated in a large-scale project involving 40,000 students from forty-two schools followed over a period of two and a half years.[4] The program has since been refined, expanded, and further evaluated with

At our school, we have seen amazing results after the first year—increased attendance, increased student achievement, and decreased incidents that lead to suspensions.

— ELEMENTARY MATH AND SCIENCE COORDINATOR

successful results in five additional large-scale projects in Norway. Since 2001, as part of the Norwegian government's plans for the prevention and reduction of delinquency and violence among children and youth, *OBPP* has been implemented on a large-scale basis in elementary and lower secondary schools throughout Norway.

Dr. Olweus has for a long time seen the phenomenon of bullying in the context of human rights.[5] As early as 1981, he proposed enacting a law against bullying in schools. He argued early that it is a fundamental human right for a student to feel safe in school and to be spared the repeated humiliation implied in bullying. In the mid-1990s, these arguments led to legislation against bullying by the Swedish and Norwegian parliaments. Similar legislation has been adopted in more than thirty states (at the date of publication) in the United States and in several other countries.

During the 1990s, Dr. Olweus worked closely with American colleagues, notably Dr. Susan P. Limber, now at Clemson University in South Carolina, to implement and evaluate the program in the United States, also resulting in positive though somewhat weaker outcomes. Since then, hundreds of schools in most every state in the United States have used the program, and the number is growing. Additional studies of these efforts are being conducted by the authors of this guide and other researchers. For summaries and citations of this research, visit www.clemson.edu/olweus. Also see the list of research articles on the Schoolwide Guide CD-ROM.

Is the *Olweus Bullying Prevention Program* a Nationally Recognized Program?

The *Olweus Bullying Prevention Program* has received recognition from a number of organizations including the following:

- Blueprints Model Program, Center for the Study and Prevention of Violence, University of Colorado at Boulder
  www.colorado.edu/cspv/blueprints/model/programs/BPP.html
- Model Program, Substance Abuse and Mental Health Services Administration, U.S. Department of Health and Human Services
  www.modelprograms.samhsa.gov
- Effective Program, Office of Juvenile Justice and Delinquency Prevention, U.S. Department of Justice
  www.ojjdp.ncjrs.org
- Level 2 Program, U.S. Department of Education
  www.helpingamericasyouth.gov

> *Note:* "Level 2" programs have been scientifically demonstrated to prevent delinquency or reduce risk and enhance protection for delinquency and other child and youth problems using either an experimental or quasi-experimental research design, with a comparison group.

For more information about the authors and other awards received for their work, see About the Authors on pages 113–115.

What Type of Support Is Available as You Implement the Program in Your School?

Since *OBPP* is a program that is implemented throughout the entire school setting, implementation takes a concerted effort on everyone's part, but the rewards will be significant. It is important that you feel supported in your efforts. If you have any questions or concerns, take advantage of the following resources:

- ***Your Certified Olweus Trainer***
  To aid in program implementation, schools are strongly encouraged to contract with an outside certified Olweus trainer or have a staff member certified as an Olweus trainer. This person will have a wealth of knowledge about the program and is available for ongoing consultation via telephone and/or Internet contact (or in person, whenever possible). Your certified Olweus trainer may also know of other schools in your region that have successfully implemented the program and could serve as a resource to you.
- **Olweus Bullying Prevention Program *Web Site***
  www.clemson.edu/olweus
  This Web site provides background information about the program, implementation strategies, training information, current evaluation research, and other related resources.
- ***Hazelden Publishing Web Site***
  www.hazelden.org/olweus
  This Web site provides background information about the program and specific information about purchasing program materials.

Stop

Before moving on to the next chapter, please take some time to watch the DVD that accompanies this Schoolwide Guide. It offers additional background information about *OBPP.*

• • •

2

Considering Implementation of the Program

WHAT YOU WILL LEARN IN CHAPTER 2	
	• what resources are needed to implement *OBPP* • the difference between *OBPP* and a curriculum • what a typical implementation schedule is for *OBPP* • the steps needed to implement the program with fidelity

OBPP is a schoolwide program that requires a high level of communication, collaboration, and "buy-in" on the part of school staff (as well as parent involvement) to be successful. *OBPP* is not a short-term solution. It is designed to be integrated into your school's daily routines and procedures over the long term.

For these reasons, implementing *OBPP* takes more time, support, and resources than some other types of bullying prevention efforts, but the outcomes of this effort can be far more significant and long-lasting.

Before any school decides to use *OBPP,* it is important to determine whether there is an adequate level of buy-in, commitment, and resources at a building level to undertake such a broad-reaching initiative.

We encourage school leaders to think through the support and resources that will be needed, and whether those resources are adequately in place to make your efforts effective. School leaders should also look at how *OBPP* fits with existing programs, the school's structure, and the school's needs. A general guideline is that a majority of your staff need to be actively participating in the program to make it effective. If, after training and motivating your staff, you feel that a majority will participate, you are probably able to move forward.

What Support Will You Have at the District Level?

Because *OBPP* is a systemwide approach to bullying, it needs not only the support of classroom teachers, key school staff, and building administrators, but also the support of district leadership as well.

District-level support may be required to ensure financial support and to reinforce implementation of the program's policies and procedures. Support from the school superintendent and the school board will also help parents, teachers, and other staff realize the importance of the program and their participation in it.

School staff will be more excited about the program if they see the administration promoting their involvement in it. As you think about adopting this program for your school, identify the type of support you will need from your district leadership and ask for it, before any investment in the program is made.

If the leadership support is not there, you may want to hold off on implementation for a time, while you educate these key leaders on the importance and benefits of the program and work to garner their active support.

You can educate your district and school leadership by showing them the Schoolwide Guide DVD, sharing with them the list of *OBPP* research articles (on the Schoolwide Guide CD-ROM; see page 6), inviting your certified Olweus trainer to meet with them, or inviting other local school leaders who have successfully implemented the program to speak to your leadership.

What Other Resources Will You Need?

If you have the active support of your district and school leadership, the next item to consider is the cost of implementing the program. From the start, you should consider not only the costs of initiating the program but also those of maintaining the program over time.

The greatest costs are incurred during initial start-up, but you will need to budget for ongoing training and other activities that will keep your staff's commitment to the program running high. As you consider these costs, keep in mind that implementing *OBPP* will most likely cut down on lost teaching time and staff burnout, protect your school from potential legal actions related to bullying, and in the long term reduce the costs to society caused by the effects of bullying on both the student who is bullied and the students who bully others.

Depending upon the size of your school, purchasing the program materials (the Schoolwide Guide and Teacher Guide) can range from $1,500 to $3,200. The Olweus Bullying Questionnaire will be a separate cost that begins at $250 for a single school using the manual entry CD-ROM format and somewhat higher for schools using the scannable version (available now) or online version (may be available in the future).

As was mentioned earlier, it is recommended that all school leaders and every member of your Bullying Prevention Coordinating Committee (BPCC) have a copy of this Schoolwide Guide and the Teacher Guide. Every teacher (or at a minimum, every three teachers) should have a copy of the Teacher Guide. (Check with a Hazelden sales representative to determine possible discounts for large-order purchases at 1-800-328-9000 or 1-651-213-4000.)

Here are some other costs to consider:

- a two-day training of the BPCC members by a certified Olweus trainer
- substitute teachers so that teachers can attend a full-day staff training (you may need to work with teacher unions to determine the rate of pay)
- supplies for your school kick-off event
- optional program promotional materials such as posters, table tents, and so on (reproducible templates are available on the Schoolwide Guide CD-ROM; see chapters 8 and 9)
- supplies such as paper to reproduce handouts, transparencies, and so on
- ongoing program evaluation costs (processing and reporting questionnaire results on an annual basis)
- a "booster" training for staff
- optional supplemental classroom support materials (including bullying-related literature or videos)

If your school implements *OBPP* as part of a large-scale districtwide or statewide effort, you may wish to have a member of the BPCC become a certified Olweus trainer who can then head up all training of existing and new staff. To become certified, this person needs to attend a three-day Olweus Training of Trainers session, attend a two-day booster training, and take part in eighteen months of telephone consultation with an Olweus training director.

Large schools or school districts may also choose to hire an OBPP coordinator who will coordinate the program throughout the year and also become a certified Olweus trainer. Information about training, training costs, and available certified Olweus trainers may be found at www.clemson.edu/olweus/training.

Because *OBPP* is a Blueprints Model Program, SAMHSA Model Program, and Effective Program for the Office of Juvenile Justice and Delinquency Prevention, federal funding is available to support schools in purchasing and implementing the program. Financial resources may also be available through school or local violence prevention programs and grants. Local law enforcement and county health departments have also financed some schools' programs. (Check with a Hazelden sales representative for assistance in obtaining funding at 1-800-328-9000 or 1-651-213-4000.)

Grant information is also available on the Schoolwide Guide CD-ROM.

Why Is a "Systems-Change" Approach Better Than a Classroom Curriculum?

Bullying problems don't just happen in the classroom, nor do they involve just the student being bullied and the students who are doing the bullying. Bullying involves and affects all students and adults in the school. Changing the school climate requires a multilevel effort that goes beyond simple classroom curriculum interventions. Bullying problems need to be solved as they happen in a consistent manner across grade levels and in all areas of the school. For this reason, prevention efforts need to reach beyond the individual classroom.

While a classroom curriculum may last a few weeks, *OBPP* is used throughout the school year and is ongoing. This is important in order to have enduring and positive effects on the prevalence of bullying and the school climate.

Although some schools have seen immediate positive effects in student behavior, many schools have found that changes occur gradually. As was mentioned earlier, for students in grades 4–7, most of the positive results can be seen after only eight months of intervention work, given reasonably good implementation of the program. For students in grades 8–10, it may take somewhat more time, maybe two years, to achieve equally good results. As you consider adopting this program, it is important that you are committed to doing it for more than one year.

The *OBPP* materials on the CD-ROM are reproducible, which helps keep down your costs. They are not designed to be grade-level specific. Teachers will adapt the materials and classroom discussions to the developmental needs of their students. Much of what makes this program successful is not dependent upon materials but on a well-trained staff that knows how to intervene in bullying situations, supervise students, and help students process and understand what bullying is, how to prevent it, and how to stop it.

The creation of a BPCC in the school also goes beyond a curriculum type of intervention. This committee, made up of school staff, teachers, administrators, and parents, acts in an advisory capacity (all members should be trained) but also ensures that every component of the program is carried out.

What Is an Optimal Timeline for Launching the Program?

You should plan to spend approximately four to six months in preparation before implementing *OBPP* in your school. This preparation is done in consultation with your certified Olweus trainer.

Below is an optimal timeline for schoolwide implementation of *OBPP,* assuming a program launch at the beginning of the fall semester. (Alternatively, but somewhat less optimally, the program could be launched just after winter break, with the Olweus Bullying Questionnaire administered the previous fall and staff trainings held in the winter.)

Although this timeline provides a general framework for program implementation, it is important for each school to implement the program at its own pace

Target Dates for Fall Launch	Activity
Late winter/ early spring	Select members of the BPCC and an on-site OBPP coordinator.
March/April	Administer the Olweus Bullying Questionnaire.
April/May	Hold a two-day training with members of the BPCC; have the committee meet every two weeks to work out the details of program implementation.
May/June	Input data (if using the manual entry version) or obtain data (if using the scannable version) of the Olweus Bullying Questionnaire; review data from the questionnaire.
August/September	Conduct a one-day training with all school staff. Also hold your school kick-off event(s) with students and parents.
Beginning of the fall semester, following the one-day staff training	Plan, schedule, and launch other elements of the schoolwide program: • Introduce school/class rules against bullying. • Begin class meetings. • Increase supervision; review and coordinate your supervisory system. • Initiate individual interventions with students. • Start regular staff discussion groups (scheduled before the school year starts). • Hold parent meetings.

and with integrity. Your school's certified Olweus trainer will help your Bullying Prevention Coordinating Committee consider a timeline that best fits your school's needs.

The Schoolwide Guide CD-ROM includes a flowchart that gives an overview of the steps needed to implement the program over time.

What Are the Challenges of Implementing This Program?

One of the biggest challenges of implementing *OBPP* is setting aside enough class time for class meetings and staff time for training and regular discussion groups.

OBPP requires that teachers hold weekly class meetings to discuss the rules about bullying and to engage students in discussions of bullying, peer relations, and other timely social issues. The length of each meeting varies depending on students' developmental level, but typically is the equivalent of a class period (for example, 15 to 30 minutes for K–2, 30 to 40 minutes for intermediate and middle school students).

Although this may seem like a large amount of class time at the outset, teachers soon see the benefits of these meetings. The benefits include increasing problem-solving behavior and decreasing relationship issues, enhancing the sense of community and positive classroom climate, and providing a forum for students to discuss incidents or issues that are important to them. Implementing *OBPP* in the classroom may actually help teachers spend more time on learning because it allows them to address social and behavior problems and climate issues in a proactive way, rather than a reactive one.

Staff discussion groups of no more than fifteen people will also need to meet regularly for approximately one hour, preferably every two weeks but at least monthly for the first year of the program and then somewhat less frequently after that. This will help ensure consistency in how the program is implemented and how bullying situations are dealt with, and provide an opportunity for staff to problem-solve together. We highly recommend setting aside time specifically for these staff discussion groups. In rare cases where schools are having particular trouble finding the time for these groups, the staff discussion groups can be incorporated into already existing meetings (such as grade-level or team-level meetings), but be sure to allow enough time to just talk about *OBPP* concepts and implementation issues.

As mentioned earlier, one way to deal with these challenges of class time and teacher time is to ensure that the program is supported by the school administration, district superintendent, and school board. Also encourage all your staff to be patient with the first steps of implementation, as the program will very quickly become part of the daily school routine.

How Do You Know When You Are Ready to Implement the Program?

You will know your school is ready to begin implementation of *OBPP* when

- There is a commitment from the school and district leadership to implement the program.
- The majority of school administrators, teachers, and non-teaching staff see bullying prevention as a priority in your school (with a majority of classroom staff committed to doing *OBPP* and with most of the remainder being open to change).
- You have funding for the materials, training, and ongoing support.
- You have leadership in your school that can serve on the BPCC.
- You have a commitment to continue the program long term. It is important that your initial plans detail how the program will be sustained for several years.
- You have talked through the program with a certified Olweus trainer so you clearly understand what it is about and what your school is committing to.

If you cannot answer "yes" to these items, we encourage you to continue to learn about the program in greater depth and to take steps to build consensus and commitment. This may include administering the Olweus Bullying Questionnaire so you can demonstrate the level of bullying in your school and the need for the program.

You may also want to take time to continue to educate your school leadership about the need. Your certified Olweus trainer can help with this. Also explore funding sources through the help of your Hazelden sales representative.

If you can say "yes" to all these items, you are ready to begin learning about the program in greater depth and begin your planning. The next chapter will help you move forward in this process.

• • •

3

Getting Started in Your School

WHAT YOU WILL LEARN IN CHAPTER 3	
	• the core principles of *OBPP* • ways schools can go wrong in addressing bullying • more about the schoolwide components of the program • more about the classroom, individual, and community components of the program

Implementing *OBPP* requires collaboration and communication among all members of a school staff. This effort can be guided by the program's core principles.

What Are the Core Principles behind the *Olweus Bullying Prevention Program?*

OBPP is based on a core set of guiding principles. These principles are derived chiefly from research on the development and modification of the problem behaviors implied in bullying, notably aggressive behavior or abusive behavior toward peers. The overarching goal is to restructure the school environment in such a way as to markedly reduce both opportunities and rewards for bullying behavior.

It is important to develop a school environment characterized by the following core principles. Understanding and abiding by these core principles will help you implement *OBPP* with integrity and success. Here is a brief overview:

PRINCIPLE 1

Warmth, Positive Interest, and Involvement Are Needed on the Part of Adults in the School

Positive interest and involvement mean many things—taking time to know students, making a special effort to help them, with homework for example, showing appropriate interest in students' personal lives, treating them with respect, and finding ways to praise them. The focus should be on developing a sense of community connection and caring, and praising the positive, supportive behavior of students, while addressing bullying situations in respectful ways.

Being positive and respectful should not be limited to teacher-student interactions, either. Students need to see teachers and other adults in school treating each other this way as well. School staff are important role models for students, and when staff work cooperatively, it sets a tone of teamwork and unity in the building.

PRINCIPLE 2

Set Firm Limits to Unacceptable Behavior

Students need a clear understanding of what your school's anti-bullying rules are and the possible consequences for breaking them. Just presenting the rules isn't enough. They need to be clarified and thoroughly discussed. In addition, these rules need to be implemented with students at each grade level so they understand in real-life terms what it means to follow the rules. The *OBPP* rules are discussed in more detail in chapter 8 of this guide.

PRINCIPLE 3

Consistently Use Nonphysical, Nonhostile Negative Consequences When Rules Are Broken

Students need to experience that the adults in your school will address bullying in roughly the same way, using the same rules and similar guidelines for use of positive and negative consequences. This creates a school climate where bullying behaviors are unacceptable and assures students who are bullied that adults will take action to stop bullying.

Positive consequences alone will not usually get aggressive students to change their behavior. However, using physical or violent punishments has been shown to increase aggression in students. Positive and negative consequences are discussed in more detail in chapter 8 of this guide.

PRINCIPLE 4

Adults in the School Should Function as Authorities and Positive Role Models

OBPP is based on an authoritative (not authoritarian) adult-student relationship model in which the adults are encouraged to be clear and visible authorities with responsibility for making sure a student's entire school experience is safe and positive. An authoritative leadership style implies a combination of positive interest and involvement on the one hand and clear expectations for appropriate behavior and firm limits to unacceptable behavior on the other.

Adults are important role models for students. As was just mentioned, the adults in the school need to model positive behavior toward each other and the students. When students see adults taking action against bullying behavior, it empowers them to do the same.

Cooperation and teamwork between adults at school sets up a model for students to follow and contributes to a positive, warm, and caring school environment. It is also important that the adults don't bully students by being sarcastic, derogatory, or disrespectful, abusing the power they have as teachers or other school staff.

What Are Some Ways Schools Can Go Wrong in Addressing Bullying?

Although well intentioned, school administrators, educators, and other staff can make the mistake of addressing bullying in the following ineffective ways:

Using Simple Short-Term Solutions (Such as One-Time Motivational Speakers)
Research has shown that effective bullying prevention programs are those that attempt to change the climate of the school and its expectations for student behavior. Preventing and stopping bullying takes the work of everyone in the school over the long term because the problem is so pervasive.

Inviting a speaker to give a one-time presentation to your student body is not effective as a stand-alone strategy against bullying and may even unfairly raise student expectations that adults will respond. However, using this type of intervention as part of a schoolwide approach can be beneficial and provide motivation to students, as long as the messages offered are consistent with *OBPP* principles.

Pursuing "Program du Jour" Approaches
Some schools look for the latest and "hottest" programs and try them out for a short period of time. Yet hopping from program to program like this does not

A school environment that's safe helps kids come ready to learn, and maybe that's why our school [which uses *OBPP*] is one of the best ever.

— A MIDDLE SCHOOL STUDENT

produce long-term change and can contribute to staff burnout and lowered commitment to a more effective approach. No program, no matter how sound, will be effective if staff refuse to use it (or refuse to use it as intended). *OBPP* has been proven to result in long-term, lasting effects if implemented consistently and with fidelity from year to year.

Providing Group Treatment for Students Who Bully

Research shows grouping together students who bully others for therapeutic reasons can have a negative effect. The students in the group tend to become role models for each other and reinforce each other's antisocial and bullying behavior.

Providing Self-Esteem Programs for Students Who Bully

OBPP research and other studies indicate that students who bully others tend to have little anxiety and uncertainty or are average in this respect. Their self-esteem is also about average or relatively positive.[1]

Working to enhance the self-esteem of such students will, therefore, do nothing to curb their bullying behavior. It may, in fact, have the undesired effect of strengthening their confidence in their position as aggressors.

Focusing on Anger-Management Training

Bullying is usually not an expression of uncontrolled anger, but proactive aggressive behavior intended to harm someone repeatedly.

Enforcing "Zero Tolerance" Policies for Bullying

These policies, also called "student exclusion" policies, were developed as tools for responding to drugs and weapons at school and generally do not include options for a graduated response. While we do want to reinforce the message to students that bullying behaviors are unacceptable, "zero tolerance" policies are ineffective for several reasons. First, the number of students who bully others is quite large. In addition, rather than reducing bullying, threats of severe punishment may actually discourage students and adults from reporting bullying incidents. Finally, options for helping students who bully to develop empathy and positive social skills are lost when schools rely on suspension or expulsion.

Providing Mediation/Conflict Resolution for Bullying

Because one of the main characteristics of bullying is an imbalance of power, it cannot be considered "normal" relational conflict between two students. Bullying is a form of peer abuse, and the student who is being bullied needs to be protected from such victimization. Because of the difference in power between the student or students who bully and the student who is being bullied, conflict resolution or peer mediation strategies should not be used to address bullying problems. For more reasons why conflict resolution should not be used, see pages 36–37 in the Teacher Guide.

Selecting Inappropriate Supplemental Materials

Some bullying curricula, books, and videos may actually reinforce stereotypes about students who bully or students who are bullied. For example, some depict students who bully as always being boys or unpopular misfits, depict students who are bullied as always having some external stigma, or show girls as cruel social manipulators or victims to be rescued.

Some resources might illustrate unreal or simplistic resolutions to bullying problems, such as expecting the student who bullies and the student who is bullied to become good friends, or promoting in-kind retaliation as a means to resolve "differences."

It is important for staff and parents to be careful consumers when evaluating children's literature, parent or adult aids, or other classroom support materials in light of *OBPP* goals and principles.

What Are the Schoolwide Components of *OBPP?*

OBPP is composed of several schoolwide components in addition to classroom, individual, and community components. Together, these make up a comprehensive systems-change program that can reduce bullying in your school.

Although we briefly covered these program components in chapter 1, a more in-depth description follows. Each component is also discussed in detail in later chapters. Here are the schoolwide components:

Bullying Prevention Coordinating Committee (BPCC)

This building-level committee is responsible for making sure all components of *OBPP* are implemented in your school. This includes coordinating the administration of the Olweus Bullying Questionnaire, providing training and program information to all teachers and other staff, coordinating *OBPP* with other programs and events in your school, obtaining feedback from staff about how the program is working, and representing the program to parents, the community, and the media.

The committee holds regular meetings and one member of the committee usually acts as the coordinator of the program. Establishing a BPCC is discussed in more detail in chapter 4 of this Schoolwide Guide.

Committee and Staff Training

Before program implementation, members of the BPCC participate in a two-day training with a certified Olweus trainer. (This trainer will also provide regular follow-up consultation services for at least twelve months.) All other school personnel, including administrators, teachers, custodians, bus drivers, lunchroom and playground supervisors, support staff, and after-school program providers attend a separate full-day training led by members of your BPCC.

Actively participating in these trainings and becoming familiar with program materials will give your teachers and other staff a good understanding of the program and provide the resources and support they will need to implement the program successfully. Training is discussed in more detail in chapter 6.

Schoolwide Administration of the Olweus Bullying Questionnaire

The Olweus Bullying Questionnaire is administered to students before the program begins and at regular (ideally yearly) intervals after that. This anonymous questionnaire is designed for students in grades 3–12.

The questionnaire results will reveal the nature and extent of bullying at your school, including aspects of the school environment that might contribute to bullying. It will provide a common definition of bullying for students, and it will help your school tailor bullying prevention efforts to the needs of your particular school community and assess how the program is working over time. Selected results can also be used in class meetings and discussions with students. Administration of the questionnaire is discussed in more detail in chapter 5.

Staff Discussion Groups

Discussion groups for teachers and other school personnel involved in *OBPP* provide another level of support and information about the program and contribute to its success. Each discussion group, of no more than fifteen people, meets for approximately one hour preferably every two weeks, but at least monthly for the first year of the program, and then somewhat less frequently after that.

These groups allow time for in-depth discussion about the program and reflection about the bullying prevention efforts at your school. Teachers will particularly find these discussions extremely helpful in learning about the program components, solving problems, and planning for how they will direct program activities in the classroom. Holding staff discussion groups is discussed in more detail in chapter 7.

Introducing School Rules and Discipline Procedures

To ensure that students receive a consistent message throughout your school, every classroom and all staff will be asked to adopt the same four anti-bullying rules. These rules should be added to your school's disciplinary handbook or policy manual. They are not meant to replace your current disciplinary system, but to provide specific guidelines for bullying. It is important that the same rules be in effect in every classroom and throughout the school.

Your school's Bullying Prevention Coordinating Committee may develop guidelines for consistent positive consequences for students who follow the rules and consistent negative consequences for students who break them. Although your school's BPCC may develop these general guidelines, how school staff members apply them will vary depending on each bullying situation.

You will need to meet with all staff to discuss these rules and procedures, including the location and use of a "time-out" room, if used; who will follow up on bullying incidents; and how teachers and staff can be consistent, yet flexible, in their use of consequences. The school rules and examples of positive and negative consequences are discussed in more detail in chapter 8.

Reviewing and Refining the Supervisory System

One of the most important tasks your BPCC will tackle is to review and refine your school's supervisory system, so that bullying is less likely to happen. An important goal of a supervisory system will be to use staff in effective ways to monitor and enforce anti-bullying rules throughout your school, and especially in "hot spots" like the playground/athletic fields, restrooms, and lunchroom. The more staff is engaged in this supervision, the more bullying will be seen and addressed, and the less likely bullying is to continue. Refining your supervisory system is discussed in detail in chapter 9.

School Kick-Off Event

Your school's BPCC will be planning an all-school kick-off event, using an assembly, skit, video, or group activity to introduce *OBPP* to students. This kick-off event will also introduce your school's anti-bullying rules and explain how bullying will be addressed throughout the school year. Teachers should have their first class meeting shortly after this event to expand on the concepts and rules that were introduced.

A kick-off event can be held just for students or can include parents too. You will want to have a kick-off event at the beginning of your program, and yearly thereafter at the beginning of each new school year as a reminder that the program is still in effect and that bullying will still be addressed in a serious way. The school kick-off event is discussed in more detail in chapter 11.

Schoolwide Parent Involvement

Parents are important partners in addressing bullying. They are involved throughout the program by attending the kick-off event (optional), coming to schoolwide parent meetings, receiving information about bullying, and, whenever possible, by attending individual classroom parent meetings. One or more parents also serve on the BPCC, providing guidance on ways to keep parents informed of program efforts through brochures, letters, newsletters, events, or online bulletin boards. Suggestions about how to engage parents in the program are provided in chapter 13.

What Are the Classroom Components of *OBPP?*

In addition to these schoolwide components, there are a number of activities that will happen at the classroom level. The following is a brief description, with more detailed descriptions available in the Teacher Guide.

Discussion and Enforcement of Schoolwide Anti-Bullying Rules

Teachers will introduce the schoolwide anti-bullying rules to their students and (where appropriate) incorporate them into their class rules, so students hear a consistent message. These rules will be discussed during class meetings, and teachers will enforce these rules with graduated positive and negative consequences. Rules will also be posted in each classroom for easy reference by teachers and students.

Class Meetings

Class meetings together with the class rules and role-playing are among the most important components of *OBPP*. The purpose of these weekly (or more frequently, as individual teachers choose) meetings is to build a sense of class cohesion and community, to teach the rules and consequences of bullying, to problem-solve, to help students understand their role in bullying situations, and to address issues about bullying as they arise.

Role-Playing

As a part of class meetings, students will participate in role-playing. Role-plays help students problem-solve and generate solutions to bullying situations. They help students develop a repertoire of actions that they can take when they are confronted with bullying situations. They also help students build empathy and perspective-taking skills by exploring the motivation and feelings of the characters in the scenarios. Guidelines on how to do role-plays effectively are provided in chapter 7 of the Teacher Guide.

Involving Parents

Teachers are encouraged to hold classroom-level parent meetings during the school year. Holding two to three such meetings during the year is ideal, but teachers may need to hold fewer, depending upon the demands on their time. These meetings help parents understand the issue of bullying, why this program is important, and the role they can play in its implementation. Meeting with parents in this way establishes a strong partnership against bullying. Additionally, having this partnership in place will be helpful if teachers need to call them later about their own child's involvement in bullying.

Ways that your BPCC can support these classroom efforts is discussed in more detail in chapter 12.

What Are the Individual Components of *OBPP?*

If a bullying problem arises, it will need to be dealt with on an individual level, both inside and outside of the classroom. Staff will receive training on how to address bullying if and when they observe it, and on how to follow up after the fact with students involved in or suspected of bullying. This means talking to the student who has been bullied to find out specific information about the incident, while providing emotional support.

Staff will also need to talk to the student or students who bullied the other student, as well as, most likely, the parents of all students involved. Another important part of this component is providing individualized support for students at risk for being bullied or for bullying others. This component is discussed in chapter 10 and is also covered in greater detail in chapter 8 of the Teacher Guide.

What Are the Community Components of *OBPP?*

It is a good idea to engage your larger community in your bullying prevention efforts. Even though the majority of bullying incidents take place on school grounds during school hours, bullying doesn't cease at the doors to your school. It occurs at school bus stops, community parks, summer camps, neighborhoods, and anywhere that children gather. Community members can help spread anti-bullying messages and efforts outside your school as well as provide support and resources to enhance your program within your school building.

Community support could include funding for the program and training or donations of needed goods for schoolwide events. Your school's BPCC should involve community members such as volunteers or workers in youth organizations (for example, youth recreation, scouting groups, or other youth clubs), city council members, county commissioners, and representatives from violence prevention coalitions, businesses, and faith-based organizations in bullying prevention efforts.

The committee will also be encouraged to examine ways to spread anti-bullying messages beyond your school's doors through the media, local governments, businesses, community nonprofit organizations, and law enforcement. Enlisting community support is another way to reinforce the message that bullying is not acceptable anywhere. For more information about how to involve your local community in your school's *OBPP* efforts, see chapter 14.

The school, classroom, individual, and, to some extent, the community interventions are all important to prevent and stop bullying. And they depend to a large extent on one another. For example, the schoolwide policies and procedures must be in place before teachers can discuss the rules and do effective interventions at the individual level.

How Do You Maintain the Fidelity of the Program?

Maintaining program fidelity is critical to achieving the success that many other schools have achieved with *OBPP*. Fidelity means implementing the program as closely as possible to the original program design. The Schoolwide Guide CD-ROM includes an *OBPP* Schoolwide Implementation Checklist for your first year of implementation to measure how well you are doing with fidelity.

Now that you are well acquainted with all of the components of *OBPP* and know what you need to do to get started, you are ready to move on to actually selecting an OBPP coordinator and creating a BPCC. This will be outlined in the next chapter.

• • •

4

Selecting a Program Coordinator and Establishing a Bullying Prevention Coordinating Committee

WHAT YOU WILL LEARN IN CHAPTER 4	
	• the steps to selecting an OBPP coordinator • the steps to selecting BPCC members • the key tasks and responsibilities of these two positions

Now that you have decided to implement *OBPP* in your school, the first thing you will need to do is select an OBPP coordinator and form a Bullying Prevention Coordinating Committee (BPCC).

Who Should You Select for the Program Coordinator Position?

The person who is selected to be your on-site OBPP coordinator could be a school counselor, school administrator, prevention specialist, teacher, or member of the non-teaching staff. Depending on the size of your school/school district and the number of schools implementing the program, this could also be a paid position. Many schools choose to have co-coordinators.

It is important that the program coordinator

- has good leadership and communication skills
- has the support of the school and district administration
- is organized
- is a good facilitator
- is able to work well with school administrators, staff, faculty, and parents and is someone school personnel respect

- is permitted by the administration to devote adequate time to program coordination
- feels passionate about the issue of bullying prevention
- is familiar with *OBPP,* is an advocate of the program, and supports its approach toward bullying prevention and intervention
- can attend a Training of Trainers (if the school district wants this individual to become a certified trainer) or can consult regularly with a certified Olweus trainer

Here are the initial tasks of the program coordinator:

1. Work with school administrators to select or recruit members of the BPCC. The school administration could identify these people for the coordinator or work with the coordinator to identify representatives. The coordinator might then contact potential members and discuss their participation on the committee. A sample letter to invite people to serve on the committee is provided on the Schoolwide Guide CD-ROM. The coordinator is encouraged to follow up this letter with a personal contact to talk more about the program and the role of the committee, so potential members understand and accept their role prior to training.
2. Assist administrators at the building and district levels as appropriate to set a date for a two-day *OBPP* training for your school's BPCC. A certified Olweus trainer should conduct this training.
3. Set up times for BPCC meetings. The committee will meet at least every two weeks for the first three months to plan the implementation of the program; after that they should meet monthly at a regular date and time. The program coordinator will need to look at the school and district calendars to make sure dates and times are available to school personnel who serve on the committee. A room will also need to be reserved for these meetings.

Note: Until a program coordinator is selected, the building administrator may take on some of these initial responsibilities for establishing the committee.

Who Should You Select to Be Bullying Prevention Coordinating Committee Members?

The BPCC will have the overarching responsibility for overseeing and planning the implementation of *OBPP* in the entire school setting. The committee has several responsibilities:

1. To make plans for implementing the various components of the program, including the administration of the Olweus Bullying Questionnaire.
2. To communicate these plans to teachers, other school staff, and parents.
3. To plan and implement the kick-off event and all other events that are part of the school program.
4. To ensure that the program is coordinated with other programs and activities at the school.
5. To obtain feedback from teachers and other staff about how the program is progressing.
6. To represent the intervention program to parents, the local community, and the media.

Each committee member is essential because he or she represents a constituent group that needs to be involved in order to make the program successful. It is the responsibility of committee members to communicate information about the program to their constituent group. For example, teachers who serve on the committee are responsible for educating other teachers at their grade level about the program.

Because this is a working committee, its members need to be task-oriented with a willingness to take on specific responsibilities for the program implementation, such as planning meetings and events and contacting teachers and parents for additional support.

It is recommended that the BPCC be composed of the following members:

- a school administrator (principal or assistant principal)
- a teacher from each grade level
- a school counselor, school psychologist, or other school-based mental health professional
- a representative of the non-teaching staff (such as a playground monitor, bus driver, cafeteria worker, custodian)
- one or two parents
- a representative from the community (if possible), such as an after-school or youth program staff member or representative from the business or faith community who might have a stake in the results of the program
- other school personnel (such as a nurse, school resource officer, Title IX representative) who may bring particular expertise to the committee

One or two student representatives may also serve on the committee. Alternatively, a separate student advisory group may be formed. Student representatives like this work best in a middle school/junior high school setting. Generally, elementary students are too young to take on this role, although they still can provide very useful input into the program.

If you do include students on your committee or in a separate advisory group, it is important that you give them meaningful roles. Students could take on the
9 job of educating other students or advising your committee on how the program should be set up so that it addresses students' concerns. Enter the names of your BPCC members on the form provided on the Schoolwide Guide CD-ROM.

Specific members of the committee will be responsible for several tasks.
10 A chart outlining these important tasks is available on the Schoolwide Guide CD-ROM.

Why Is the Bullying Prevention Coordinating Committee Important?

Because *OBPP* is a schoolwide program, it takes schoolwide coordination to make it succeed. That is why it is important to establish a motivated coordinating committee to take a leadership role, right from the beginning of the program. This committee can bring together all the key players, build consensus and support for the program, and plan the program's implementation.

Having a strong and representative committee also ensures that the important tasks can be tackled in an organized and unified way. There are too many tasks that need to be done for one person to take them on by himself or herself. In addition, experience shows that when a school's *OBPP* efforts hinge on the charisma or efforts of only one or two key people, the school's efforts are likely to fall apart over time.

Forming a committee with diverse and varied members allows for a variety of perspectives and ideas to come forth. For example, parents bring a perspective to the bullying issue that is different from the perspective teachers bring. All voices and ideas need to be heard.

Typically, committees range in size from eight to fifteen members depending on the composition of the school. Carefully consider the makeup and size of your committee. If committees are too small, they may not adequately represent the many important voices at your school. If they are too large, it may be difficult to find times to meet and for members to feel ownership of the program.

What Should You Do at Your BPCC Meetings?

At least three months before kicking off the program with students, your BPCC members should participate in a two-day training with your certified Olweus trainer. After the training, your BPCC will likely want to meet at least every other week until implementation with students begins. Your program coordinator should work with your school administration to facilitate these meetings.

During these initial bimonthly meetings, members will review all program materials and determine how all aspects of the program will be integrated into your school. This includes scheduling administration dates for the Olweus Bullying Questionnaire, determining staff training dates, refining your supervisory system, incorporating *OBPP* rules and concepts into your school's discipline policy, ordering materials, and planning schoolwide events.

The committee should work to actively involve as many adults as possible in the school in *OBPP*. Establishing BPCC subcommittees may also be helpful in order to accomplish tasks and engage as many members as possible.

You will find a copy of a BPCC workbook on the Schoolwide Guide CD-ROM. Each member of the committee should be given a copy of this workbook for use during these initial meetings. As mentioned earlier, it is recommened that each committee member also have a copy of this Schoolwide Guide and a copy of the Teacher Guide. Both will be referred to throughout your planning process.

Although every school's committee will work at a different pace and on different tasks, we have provided a sample agenda and outline for your first committee meeting on the Schoolwide Guide CD-ROM.

At subsequent meetings it is recommended that you work through the workbook together as a committee. While your workbook will be updated over time, your goal will be to address all the issues outlined there before the start of the program with students.

Once the program is up and running, the BPCC should continue to meet monthly to discuss how the program is going and to take care of any problems or issues that arise. A sample agenda for these ongoing monthly meetings is also included on the Schoolwide Guide CD-ROM.

During these ongoing meetings, it is important to consider how to keep the program visible and consistent throughout the school year. You will also need to think of how you can continue to promote the program to students and staff.

On a yearly basis, discuss who wants to remain on the committee, what new members are needed, and what additional training is needed for new and returning members. In general, it is a good idea to rotate membership on this committee, both to avoid wearing out committee members and to gain new ideas and perspectives. Do this in a staggered way, so you always retain a few members to provide continuity.

How Can You Recognize and Reward Your BPCC Members?

The BPCC members will be asked to contribute a great deal of time and energy to the program. It is important that their efforts are recognized in some way by school administration, staff, and teachers. This recognition could come in the form of refreshments during meetings, special coffee mugs, certificates of appreciation, CEUs (continuing education units) for being involved in *OBPP* trainings, stipends for extra hours spent, or mentions in the school newsletter or other publications. Keeping the members of this ongoing committee motivated to continue overseeing the program is critical to its success.

Maintaining a motivated committee also entails providing opportunities for members to take ownership of the program. Members' ideas and contributions need to be heard and acted upon. The program coordinator should give all committee members tasks and responsibilities, so they are fully participating.

• • •

5

Administering the Questionnaire and Using the Results

WHAT YOU WILL LEARN IN CHAPTER 5	
	• the benefits of administering the Olweus Bullying Questionnaire • about the Olweus Bullying Questionnaire and how to administer it • how to use the questionnaire results in your program planning and administration

One of the first things you will need to do is find out the prevalence of bullying in your school by administering the Olweus Bullying Questionnaire to students in grades 3 and higher. The questionnaire should be administered annually at the same time of year to monitor changes in bullying behavior and to evaluate the effectiveness of your bullying prevention efforts. The results will help you plan and modify your program as needed.

Currently the Olweus Bullying Questionnaire is available as a scannable version or on a CD-ROM with manual data entry. The manual version is less expensive but will take more time to implement, particularly if you have large numbers of students filling out the questionnaire. An online version is also being considered and may be available soon.

Why Survey Students about Bullying?

Surveying students about bullying can help your school's efforts by

- obtaining detailed and reliable information on bullying behavior, attitudes, and related issues in the school environment, thereby increasing awareness and motivation on the part of school staff and parents to address bullying at school

- providing information critical to planning your bullying prevention efforts and to redesigning supervision in specific areas of your school
- providing baseline data from which to measure progress in reducing bullying

What Is the Olweus Bullying Questionnaire?

The Olweus Bullying Questionnaire is a standardized, validated questionnaire. It is imperative that it be administered anonymously. Students will be asked to identify how adults at school have responded to bullying in the past, and they will be more likely to answer honestly if they believe their teacher or other school staff members will not know how individual students have answered. Research has shown that this self-reporting survey is an accurate instrument in measuring the levels of bullying in a school setting.

This multiple-choice questionnaire addresses the following:

- How frequently are students in our school bullying or being bullied?
- What types of bullying are most common?
- Where does bullying occur?
- How often do students report bullying? To whom?
- How do students feel about bullying?
- How responsive do they feel adults are to bullying at school?

The questionnaire also provides a definition of bullying that will then be understood by students throughout the course of the program. Many questions are aligned with particular components of *OBPP* so the results give you specific planning information to help you monitor and improve upon your program efforts.

The questionnaire is not designed for use with students below the third grade. However, if teachers in grade 2 or lower would like to use the questionnaire, we recommend it be used in the following ways:

- The teacher could read selected questions aloud and explain their meaning. Then students could fill in a shortened answer sheet with direction from the teacher.
- Alternatively, teachers could record answers using a group-response format by asking the question and having students raise their hands or use another simple means of response. If you are using these less confidential methods, care should be taken not to put students "on the spot," and teachers should be alert to students' tendencies to respond like their friends or with the majority.

- The teacher could use several questions as discussion starters for class meetings. A question could be read and then time could be allowed for students to share their ideas and experiences.

We encourage you to discuss these options with your certified Olweus trainer before recommending them to teachers. It is also recommended that the questionnaire be read to students with limited reading ability, learning difficulties, or limited English literacy skills. The questionnaire is available in both English and Spanish.

What Is the Process of Administering the Olweus Bullying Questionnaire?

With the purchase of either the scannable version or manual version of the Olweus Bullying Questionnaire, schools will receive detailed instructions on how to administer the questionnaire and obtain the results. Following the instructions as closely as possible ensures that the questionnaire is administered as designed.

The questionnaire should be administered to students no earlier than six to eight weeks after the summer or winter break. Many questions ask students to reflect on their experiences with peers since the beginning of the school year (or alternatively since the winter break), and it is important that students have at least six to eight weeks to settle into routines at school before answering these questions.

The questionnaire should be administered at the same time (same month) in subsequent years in order to obtain the same "snapshot in time" of student behavior. Following this procedure will allow you to compare results from one year to the next reliably.

All students should be surveyed on the same day and ideally at the same time to minimize discussion about the questionnaire among students before all have completed it. It is preferred that students fill out the questionnaire entirely in one sitting, although other arrangements may need to be made for students with special needs. The Olweus Bullying Questionnaire Tracking Log on the Schoolwide Guide CD-ROM can help you keep track of your administration of the questionnaire.

14

Schools should allow approximately one class period (approximately 45 minutes) for students to complete the questionnaire. Again, this timing may need to be adjusted for students with special needs.

Before administering the questionnaire, obtain any necessary consent from parents according to your district's requirements. Most schools are able to obtain "passive parental consent" (notifying parents of the school's plans to administer the questionnaire and asking that they notify the school if they do not wish their child to participate).

How Will You Analyze the Data from the Questionnaire?

If the scannable version is administered, schools will send the completed questionnaires to Hazelden Publishing for scanning and report generating. Schools will then receive detailed reports with narrative that helps interpret the results, along with graphs that highlight key results in a more visual form. These graphs can be used for presentations with stakeholders such as school staff, parents, your school board, and community members. Data from one school or one school district will also be compared to a national database of other schools that have administered the questionnaire.

If the manual-entry version is purchased, the accompanying statistical software program makes it possible for a layperson to manually enter the data into the program and then analyze and interpret the results. This program is PC-compatible (not Mac-compatible) with Windows 95 through XP.

With either the scannable version or the manual entry version, a detailed profile of key data for each school (or school district), in part divided by gender and grade level, is produced.

How Do We Interpret and Use the Results?

Your school's results on the Olweus Bullying Questionnaire will help you plan your bullying prevention program to meet the specific needs of your school and will help you monitor effectiveness in subsequent years. Be sure to send a copy of the questionnaire results to your certified Olweus trainer, who will provide additional assistance in interpreting the findings and discussing possible actions to take to address the findings.

As will be discussed in chapter 16, some of the findings from the questionnaire are not likely to change over time (for example, the most common forms of bullying, the gender and grade level of students who bully), while others likely will change as a result of the program (for example, students' perceptions of teacher responsiveness to bullying).

Also be sure to compare changes in data with appropriate grade levels. For example, from year to year you should compare the data on fifth-graders in one year with fifth-graders in the next year. Because of development changes in students (for example, being bullied tends to lessen as students get older), you should not compare changes in the same group of students over several years.

The results of the questionnaire should answer the following types of questions:

- How many students are bullied at your school? How do these bullying experiences vary for boys and girls and for students in different grades?
- How many students have been bullied for a long period of time (that is, a year or more)?
- How many students are fearful of being bullied?
- Have bullied students told anyone about their experiences? If so, whom?
- How many students bully others at your school? How does this behavior vary for boys and girls and for students in different grades?
- What types of bullying are most prevalent in your school?
- What are the "hot spots" for bullying at your school?
- What are students' attitudes toward bullying at school?
- How do students feel about the reliability of adults intervening in bullying situations?
- How do students feel about the reliability of their classmates intervening in bullying situations?
- How satisfied are students with school?

These and other questions will be addressed in a variety of ways, including BPCC work, class meetings, staff trainings, and staff discussion groups. For most of these questions, you will be able to examine gender and grade differences in students' responses.

The results of the Olweus Bullying Questionnaire should first be shared with the BPCC members, so they can begin to establish school policies and procedures and refine your school's supervisory system. We then recommend sharing at least key results of the questionnaire with staff at your full-day staff training. The results can help staff realize how prevalent bullying is and how important this intervention is to the school and the well-being of all students. Staff discussion groups are a good place to further explore the results, as you focus staff efforts in the classroom and throughout your school.

Sharing select results with parents and the community can raise awareness and understanding about how your school will be working to safeguard all students, and provides a forum for presenting plans for the intervention. This can improve parental support and participation.

A word of caution, however: Consider the focus you would like to present to your community if the media reports your data. Rather than calling attention to problems, you may wish to spend more time talking about the solutions and the proactive approach your school is taking.

In many cases, it may be useful and appropriate to share general information about the questionnaire results with students. As with sharing information with parents and community members, use this as an opportunity to talk about what the adults will do to address bullying, and for students to brainstorm and work on ways they can help as well.

• • •

6

Training Your Committee and Other School Staff

WHAT YOU WILL LEARN IN CHAPTER 6	
	• the importance of training BPCC members, teachers, and other staff • the steps to take in training BPCC members • the steps to take in training all other staff

Training the BPCC, teachers, and all other school staff is key to the success of the program. Training helps ensure implementation with fidelity. Schools that have been most successful in preventing bullying have been committed to training their administrators, teachers, and other staff and committed to implementing all the components of the program.

Because *OBPP* is not a curriculum, but a comprehensive schoolwide approach, it is important that those overseeing and planning the program, as well as those implementing the program on a day-to-day basis, have a deep understanding of the issue of bullying and how to prevent it. Changing the school climate is a large task that needs to be undertaken in a systematic way.

All members of the school community need to work together to make this happen. Adults who are going to intervene in bullying situations need specific direction, since the failure to intervene is often associated with simply not knowing what to do. Training will facilitate their ability to recognize bullying and intervene when it happens.

As you prepare for your training events, it is suggested that you also plan for substitute teachers and other support staff. You may need to reserve them ahead of time and include this expense in your program budget. If you have a pool of regular substitute teachers, arrange to train them at another time as well.

Who Should Lead Your School's Trainings?

It is highly recommended that schools contract with a certified Olweus trainer who can prepare and facilitate trainings for your BPCC members. Instead of hiring an outside trainer, your school district may instead choose to send a school staff member to an *OBPP* Training of Trainers event to become a certified Olweus trainer. Details about the training can be found at www.clemson.edu/ olweus/ training.html.

What Type of Training Should the Bullying Prevention Coordinating Committee Receive?

Since the BPCC will be overseeing the program in your school, it is extremely important that all members of the committee attend a two-day training conducted by your certified Olweus trainer. BPCC members will be recognized as resident bullying prevention experts within your school, so they need to acquire the knowledge and strategies to address bullying and have the ongoing assistance from their certified Olweus trainer to sustain their efforts.

BPCC members should commit to attending the entire training (that is, not coming and going from the training session) so they do not miss any information. 15 The BPCC Two-Day Training Log on the Schoolwide Guide CD-ROM will help you keep track of the committee members that have been trained.

Even though it may be inconvenient, the lead administrator for the school building should attend the entire training as well. Experience in implementation has shown that when school administrators miss even portions of this training, they often do not develop the knowledge and skills that will enable them to best support their teachers and other staff in implementing the program. In addition, it sends the unfortunate message to other BPCC members and staff that full attention and commitment to the effort is not required. When the BPCC is not supported by building-level administration, the program likely will struggle to be successful.

It is often beneficial to hold the training away from school, so BPCC members are not called away to take care of other responsibilities, and there are no interruptions. If you must hold it at your school, meet in a part of the school where participants can be free of distractions.

The following is an overview of the learning objectives for the BPCC training. Participants will understand, based on current research,

- what bullying is and how it differs from other acts of aggression among children and youth

- the reasons why educators should be concerned about bullying
- facts and myths about the nature and prevalence of bullying
- characteristics of students involved in bullying problems
- risk factors for bullying

They will also

- understand current bullying problems at their school, using results from the administration of the Olweus Bullying Questionnaire
- become familiar with
    a. the research and philosophy behind *OBPP*
    b. the goals of *OBPP*
    c. components of the program at the schoolwide, classroom, individual, and community levels
    d. ways to maintain fidelity to the program
- learn skills and strategies to
    a. hold class meetings with students
    b. effectively intervene on the spot to address bullying
    c. follow up with students who are involved in bullying problems
    d. work with parents of students who are involved in bullying problems
    e. train members of the entire school staff in *OBPP*
- begin to develop a detailed plan to implement *OBPP* in their school

What Type of Training Should All Other School Staff Receive?

It is suggested that teachers, professional non-teaching staff, and all other school staff attend a full-day training (this could be done in two half-day blocks). Ideally, all other staff (such as cafeteria workers, custodians, playground aides, and bus drivers) will be included in this training as well. However, because these positions often have contractual constraints on people's time, we recommend that (at a minimum) they attend a half-day training that covers basic information about bullying and *OBPP,* to be followed by specialized training that meets their particular needs.

Training for all staff should be led by members of the BPCC. The process of training others will strengthen/reinforce your BPCC's role as resident bullying experts and as sources of ongoing information about bullying and *OBPP*. This will establish a leadership role for the BPCC that is critical to the success of the program.

The objectives for the all-staff training are as follows:

- to provide a basic understanding of the problem of bullying
- to provide a basic understanding of the need for a systems-change approach rather than a curriculum
- to provide knowledge about your school's bullying problem, using results from your administration of the Olweus Bullying Questionnaire
- to provide an overview of *OBPP*
- to train teachers in the implementation of the classroom components of the program
- to refine your supervisory system in your school
- to train all administrators, educators, and school staff on how to intervene in bullying situations at the individual level
- to explore successful ways to work with parents around bullying issues

What Kind of Room Arrangements and Materials Do You Need for This Staff Training?

Every school has its own space constraints; however, people will learn more and be more responsive when the training environment is comfortable and pleasant. So, look for well-lit rooms with good climate control, comfortable seating, and enough space for participants to work in both large and small groups. Be sure to have all equipment and materials ready in advance and attend to "creature comforts" (provide adequate breaks, balance sitting and listening with active learning opportunities).

The following materials will also be needed:

- Schoolwide Guide DVD and a TV with DVD player
- an LCD projector, screen, and laptop computer if PowerPoint will be used (An OBPP PowerPoint presentation is available through your certified Olweus trainer.)
- copies of the Teacher Guide (preferably one per staff, but at least one per group of three teachers)
- copies of school materials—such as the Olweus Bullying Questionnaire results, rules, policies, and procedures

16 A sample agenda for the full-day staff training is available on the Schoolwide Guide CD-ROM.

What Kind of Record Keeping and Ongoing Training Should You Do?

It is important to keep a record of the school staff who have been trained. There is an All-Staff Training Log on the Schoolwide Guide CD-ROM for this purpose. 17 The BPCC will also need to make sure that new teachers, long-term substitutes, and other new staff receive adequate training on the program. In addition, trained administrators, educators, and other staff need to mentor new employees on a yearly basis to keep the program vital.

The staff discussion groups (discussed in the next chapter) provide opportunities for discussion and problem-solving of bullying issues and *OBPP* topics. Members of the BPCC can serve as trainers during these staff discussion group meetings.

As the program progresses, the need to address specific issues in a training session will probably arise. Find ways to use these issues as learning opportunities within your staff discussion groups. Offering "booster" training days annually around particular topics of interest or need can also be helpful.

Explore what other options are available to share information about *OBPP* topics or concerns, or to share progress and ideas. For example, brief training updates could be presented at school staff meetings. These 15- to 20-minute presentations could address very specific bullying issues such as ways to recruit parents to help with class meetings, types of interventions to use with students who bully others, use of positive and negative consequences, or use of the time-out room.

Because *OBPP* is a systems-change program that continues throughout the year, it will be important to keep it visible and at the forefront of your staff's minds all year long. Frequent trainings and updates will remind teachers and all other staff of the program and improve the work they are doing.

• • •

7

Holding Staff Discussion Groups

WHAT YOU WILL LEARN IN CHAPTER 7	
	• why staff discussion groups are an important part of *OBPP* • how to find time to hold staff discussion groups • guidelines for conducting these groups

As teachers and other staff embark on implementing *OBPP,* they will need regular support and guidance about program principles and materials, effective strategies, and opportunities to talk about intervention efforts (successes and challenges). Staff discussion groups provide a regular opportunity to reinforce the *OBPP* initiative in your school.

What Are the Goals of Staff Discussion Groups?

The goals of staff discussion groups are

- to provide more detailed and comprehensive information on the intervention program and its various components
- to provide an opportunity for staff to share ideas, ask questions, and practice solutions to various problem situations in a secure environment
- to stimulate faster implementation of the various components of the program
- to share experiences and viewpoints with others in similar situations and to learn from others' positive and negative experiences
- to create and maintain motivation and commitment
- to stimulate cooperation among staff and coordination of program components and activities (to develop a whole-school policy)

How Should the Staff Discussion Groups Be Organized?

Each staff discussion group should have at least four and no more than fifteen adults. Although these groups will most likely consist of teachers, they can also include other staff who have a need for more detailed information and understanding of *OBPP*, such as non-teaching staff and after-school program staff. School administrators (principal and assistant principal) should also participate in a group. Depending on the size of your school, you will most likely need to set up more than one staff discussion group.

It is recommended that the staff discussion groups meet regularly for approximately one hour at a fixed time, ideally every two weeks but at least monthly for the first year of the program, and then somewhat less frequently after that. We highly recommend that these groups meet during a separate, regularly scheduled time. If it is difficult to schedule these as separate meetings, time could be set aside during regular staff or team meetings, but make sure adequate time is allowed for *OBPP* discussions.

It is important that the meetings last long enough to provide time for in-depth discussion and reflection. Your OBPP coordinator should try to schedule these meetings well in advance, so they are on the calendar for the school year. Early scheduling also makes it less likely that the meetings will conflict with other school events. Ideally, eight to ten meetings per group should be held during the first school year.

It is also important that appropriate rooms be reserved for the discussion groups, so meetings can take place without disturbances or interruptions. It is recommended that participation in these discussion groups be conducted during "paid time" to ensure implementation of this important OBPP activity.

The staff discussion groups should continue during the second year of implementation on a more irregular basis, but if there are new staff members at the school, a group for them could be offered more often.

Many schools find that these discussion groups are a good tool for raising and solving a variety of problems at school. For this reason, continuing more frequent meetings may be a good idea to address topics other than bullying.

Who Should Lead the Staff Discussion Groups?

It is recommended that grade-level teachers on the BPCC and the on-site OBPP coordinator lead the staff discussion groups. Generally these teachers lead a discussion group with teachers from their grade or team level. If additional staff discussion group leaders are needed at a school, this role could be filled by other BPCC members or other staff members who participated in the two-day training (for example, the nurse or school resource officer). The leader will need to feel comfortable leading discussions and role-plays with his or her colleagues and have credibility with them.

Consider having two people co-lead a discussion group. In such a situation, these two people determine how they would like to share this leadership responsibility. It is helpful, if time allows, to have one person, perhaps the OBPP coordinator, participate in all the groups, at least at the beginning of the program, to ensure coordination and communication across the various groups.

The success of these group meetings will largely depend on how well the material is presented and discussed in the groups. For this reason, it is essential that the leaders set aside time to prepare for the meetings and follow up on any issues that arise.

What Is the Impact of the Staff Discussion Groups on School Climate?

Staff discussion groups will help teachers and other staff become more invested in and excited about the program. Their involvement in these groups will help them feel supported. Meeting regularly with their colleagues will also ensure that all components of the program are being implemented consistently.

It is important for students to know that their actions will be treated the same by all of the teachers and other staff, and not just one or two. This unity will send the message to students who bully that their behavior will not go without consequences and to students who are bullied that adults in the school will help them.

What Are Some Possible Staff Discussion Topics?

The initial focus of the discussion groups should be on reading through and discussing each chapter of the Teacher Guide, as well as the resources on the Teacher Guide CD-ROM. The discussion group leaders can also take advantage of ongoing consultation with your school's certified Olweus trainer to address any other questions or issues that come up.

To begin with, your discussion groups should discuss one to two chapters from the Teacher Guide per meeting. Because time is limited, it is suggested that people read through the two chapters to be discussed ahead of time.

18 One possible outline for staff discussion group meetings is provided on the Schoolwide Guide CD-ROM.

Initially, there are key *OBPP* basics to address. Be sure to thoroughly cover how class meetings should be handled and what topics should be discussed. Also, carefully discuss how individual interventions should be handled. Review the refinements you have made to your school's supervisory system and the important roles staff will have in making sure a strong supervisory system is in place and effective.

Once a discussion group has reviewed all the chapters in the Teacher Guide, the group can move on to other bullying-related topics, such as the following:

1. Dealing with the differences in bullying among girls and boys
2. What to do when a student or students who bully dominate class meetings
3. How to deal with particular "hot spots" in your school
4. Working with non-teaching staff to prevent bullying
5. Cyber-bullying
6. How to keep each other informed of bullying problems
7. How to respond positively to specific bullying incidents or problems that arise in program implementation
8. Checking for consistency among participants in the use of positive and negative consequences for following/not following your school's anti-bullying rules
9. How to recognize and address serious issues such as sexual harassment, disability harassment, hazing, and other behaviors that may require special responses by law

19 Plan to have staff fill out a Staff Discussion Group Log (available on the Schoolwide Guide CD-ROM) for each group. You may want to collect these periodically so you have a record of what is happening in your school's discussion groups.

• • •

8

Introducing School Bullying Rules and Consequences

WHAT YOU WILL LEARN IN CHAPTER 8	
	• the four anti-bullying rules and their meaning • appropriate positive and negative consequences to use with these rules • how to introduce these rules and consequences schoolwide

One of the main objectives of *OBPP* is to create a safer and more caring school community that is free of bullying. An important step toward achieving this is by introducing four anti-bullying rules and applying positive and negative consequences to reinforce these rules. More detailed information on this topic is provided in chapter 5 of the Teacher Guide.

Begin by finding out what laws, policies, or regulations currently exist in your district or state. These may influence or inform the process your BPCC uses in implementing rules and disciplinary procedures at your school. Contact your state Department of Education as well as your district superintendent and board of education to determine what policies and procedures are already in place to specifically address bullying behaviors. If you are part of an independent school network, find out what policies your association may have in place.

What Are the Elements of a Good School District Policy?

As you consider how to address bullying behavior, explore the development of a schoolwide, but preferably a districtwide, policy on bullying. Elements of a good policy include

- a clear definition of bullying 1
- a focus on prevention 2

- the use of the *OBPP's* four anti-bullying rules (discussed in this chapter)
- the use of negative consequences for bullying and positive consequences for prosocial behavior or active bystander efforts
- procedures for reporting bullying, including the process for reporting and responding
- procedures for intervening and addressing bullying as it occurs and when it is reported (procedures are outlined in the Teacher Guide)
- procedures for working with parents when bullying problems occur (also discussed in the Teacher Guide)
- district-level standards for logical consequences and disciplinary actions
- district-level policies for handling disputes and incidents that cross the line into illegal behaviors such as assault, sexual harassment, disability harassment, hazing, and discrimination

20 A list of state anti-bullying policies that are available on the Internet is provided on the Schoolwide Guide CD-ROM.

How Do You Create Expectations That Bullying Should Not Occur?

The four core principles of *OBPP* should be used as guides in developing your anti-bullying policies and procedures. Here are those principles (discussed earlier in chapter 3):

1. Warmth, positive interest, and involvement by adults
2. Firm limits to unacceptable behavior
3. Consistent use of nonphysical, nonhostile negative consequences when rules are broken
4. Adults who function as authorities and positive role models

The first important step in establishing and integrating these principles into the fabric of your school is setting expectations for acceptable behavior on the part of all members of the school community.

What Are the Four Anti-Bullying Rules Schools Should Use to Address Bullying?

Most likely your school already has some general rules regarding student conduct. It is very important, however, that your school also adopt rules specifically about bullying. *OBPP* recommends adopting four anti-bullying rules for the entire school and each classroom. These rules have been carefully developed to effectively address different aspects of bullying. For this reason, they should not be replaced or modified, except for minor word changes in rules 2–4.

Here are the four anti-bullying rules:

1. We will not bully others.
2. We will try to help students who are bullied.
3. We will try to include students who are left out.
4. If we know that somebody is being bullied, we will tell an adult at school and an adult at home.

These rules cover both direct and more indirect forms of bullying, including social isolation and exclusion from the peer group. Even though it is a good strategy to word rules in a positive rather than a negative way (to emphasize what one can or should do rather than what one should not do), this is not a good idea with bullying. In *OBPP,* it is critical to communicate very clearly that bullying is not acceptable behavior. This is accomplished, among other ways, through the negatively worded rule 1. Rules 2–4 are worded more positively.

There is a difference between ordinary school procedural rules or ground rules—regarding concerns such as classroom etiquette, dress codes, and general safety (for example, no running in the halls)—and rules against bullying, which concern fundamental human rights.

It should be made very clear that rule 4, about reporting bullying, does not apply only to other students who are bullied. It also applies to situations where a student is being bullied himself or herself. This means, quite concretely: If I am bullied, I will tell an adult at school and an adult at home.

With every classroom and all staff members following the same rules, they are easier to enforce and students know more clearly what behavior is expected. This common set of rules sends a signal to students, parents, and others that your school has a unified and coordinated policy against bullying. These rules will be an independent part of your school's discipline policy.

Post the rules in high-traffic areas around your school, such as classrooms, the cafeteria, restrooms, the gym, near water fountains, or on buses. (Posters of the four anti-bullying rules are available on the Schoolwide Guide CD-ROM in both English and Spanish. The CD-ROM includes a color and black-and-white file of each poster. See page 60.)

These rules are not meant to replace other school rules or classroom ground rules for behavior. Rather, they are intended to supplement these rules by specifically addressing bullying behaviors.

Here is a brief overview of the four rules. More detailed descriptions are available in chapter 5 of the Teacher Guide.

RULE 1

We Will Not Bully Others

This is the most important anti-bullying rule. It should not be excluded or substantially altered. It sends a clear message to students that bullying is not acceptable in your classrooms or any area of your school. It is your staff's responsibility to introduce the rule to students, make sure students understand what it means very concretely, and explain how the rule will be enforced. Discuss this rule with students in your school's kick-off event and in class meetings using role-plays or watching the Teacher Guide DVD scenarios.

When staff members see a student or students bullying another student, they should refer to this rule. Indeed, the adults in your school must assume the primary responsibility for introducing, clarifying, exercising, supervising, and enforcing rule 1, as well as the other anti-bullying rules. It is important to note that rule 1 focuses on the behavior of the students who bully. The remaining three *OBPP* rules focus on the behavior of the students who are bullied or bystanders in bullying situations.

RULE 2

We Will Try to Help Students Who Are Bullied

This rule stresses the importance of students taking a stand against bullying and siding with those who are being bullied. This attitude can be expressed in such behaviors as finding an adult to help intervene in a situation or actively defending the student who is being bullied (if this does not entail a risk of physical injury). It may also imply becoming a friend to the bullied student and clearly and openly refusing to participate in bullying behavior.

Through the Olweus Bullying Questionnaire, we found out that our kids wanted to help but weren't sure how to do so when someone was being bullied. The *Olweus Bullying Prevention Program* has given them the tools necessary to intervene, and they think it's cool to be known as a protector.

— ELEMENTARY SCHOOL COUNSELOR

Following this rule also can mean assisting or responding to the student who was bullied after the fact to provide comfort or social support. Exactly how particular students respond in any situation will depend on factors such as their age and size, gender, and social standing in their peer group.

Through class meeting discussions and role-plays, teachers can help students develop a repertoire of appropriate actions to take in bullying situations and relationships. This rule reinforces the norm of caring for others that helps build a more positive community in your school.

RULE 3

We Will Try to Include Students Who Are Left Out

This rule is particularly designed for students who are exposed to indirect forms of bullying, such as intentional exclusion from the peer group. It is not uncommon to have one or more students in a classroom who are left out of social activities with others.

The goal of this rule is to promote the idea that, even though we may not all be friends, everyone in school is part of our circle of caring, and social exclusion is not acceptable. Simply stated, this rule means that "everyone should have someone to be with."

Encourage your teachers to lead their students in discussions about how to include classmates who are left out of activities, games, and group tasks in class, during the school day, and outside of school.

RULE 4

If We Know That Somebody Is Being Bullied, We Will Tell an Adult at School and an Adult at Home

This rule emphasizes the importance of telling an adult if students know that someone else is being bullied. As mentioned earlier, this rule also applies to the student himself or herself. They should know that: If I am bullied, I will tell an adult at school and an adult at home.

This rule is based on the fact that a considerable number, 30 to 60 percent, of students who are bullied do not tell an adult about it, neither at school nor at home.[1] Even fewer students who witness bullying tell adults. Clearly, there is a great need for more open communication regarding bullying problems among students. Rule 4 has been created specifically to stimulate such communication. To some extent, this rule overlaps with rule 2—a natural way of helping students is to tell adults. However, rule 4 amplifies and extends beyond rule 2.

Your school's enforcement of the rules about bullying and the immediate action you take when confronted with information about a bullying situation will assure students that the problem will not go unnoticed if they tell an adult. It is extremely important that the adults at your school take such information seriously and follow up with investigations and intervention measures until the problem has been solved.

Students often do not tell adults about being bullied because they see it, or are afraid that others will see it, as "tattling." Make sure students understand that this is not tattling—it is simply following an anti-bullying rule that has been adopted by your school. To tell someone about bullying is thus something that is desired and prescribed by the adults at school. It is a very important prerequisite to creating a school environment with little or no bullying.

Outlines for classroom discussions of the rules are provided on the Teacher Guide CD-ROM. Teachers are also encouraged to discuss the rules through role-playing or the use of children's literature and to make connections between school rules and other rules (at home and in society) that help us get along.

How Do You Integrate These Rules into Your Current Discipline Policy?

These rules should be incorporated into your school's behavior code, parent handbooks, and discipline policies. They should be included in student handbooks or behavior contracts. These rules should also be incorporated into every classroom's rules that teachers set for their students.

A cornerstone of *OBPP* is that adults respond, and that students expect them to respond, to bullying in a consistent way. Otherwise students will quickly learn when, and with whom, they can break the rules without consequences. To act with such consistency, teachers and all staff must clearly understand what constitutes bullying. You will want to thoroughly define both bullying and these rules during your staff training sessions. Also during staff discussion groups, teachers and other staff can practice what to do when students break the rules—how they will react and apply consequences swiftly and appropriately.

Although bullying is often implicitly part of a school's rules, it often is not explicitly named or discussed in all of its forms. It is important that your school uses the *OBPP* rules that are specific to bullying. This will make it easier for adults at the school to refer to these rules and issue positive or negative consequences for following or breaking them. Having specific rules pertaining to bullying will also make it very clear to the students that bullying is an important issue that won't be tolerated.

The BPCC will want to consider strategies for introducing and integrating the four anti-bullying rules and their consequences into your school routines and policies. Here are some good ways of doing this:

- posting reminders about the rules in your school newsletter
- posting the four anti-bullying rules poster
- laminating the rules poster and posting it on the playground
- posting magnetized rules on school buses
- asking for feedback from staff during staff discussion groups and inviting them to share their experiences with enforcing the rules and their consequences
- rewarding students (as appropriate) who help students who are bullied or make special efforts to include students who are easily left out or bullied

What Should Be the Consequences for Following or Not Following the Rules?

Once the four anti-bullying rules are introduced, staff should establish positive consequences for following rules 2–4, and negative consequences for breaking rule 1. Some schools may decide to use consistent consequences throughout the school. However, it is encouraged, whenever possible, to give staff suggestions about what would be appropriate positive and negative consequences, but leave it up to staff to implement these consequences in ways that seem appropriate to the individual situation.

Note: Although these positive and negative consequences were developed for bullying behavior, they can also be used for any antisocial or undesirable behaviors.

For a more detailed overview of both positive and negative consequences and the types of behavior that would warrant either, see pages 57–62 in the Teacher Guide.

Who Should Handle Discipline Problems Related to Bullying?

The expectation of *OBPP* is that any adult in your school should be equipped to respond to bullying behavior on the spot. Your BPCC training will include strategies and techniques for helping staff practice using effective intervention strategies. Sometimes, this level of intervention may be enough to stop a student's bullying behavior.

However, in situations requiring more complex consequences or when follow-up is needed with students, we recommend, whenever possible, that the primary classroom teacher or another staff member who has a close relationship with the student (such as a homeroom teacher, an advisor, or a lead teacher, if in middle school/junior high school) be involved in establishing and enforcing bullying consequences. This staff member often has the strongest relationship with the student and the most daily contact. It will be easier for this person to enforce consequences and do so in a caring way.

If a bullying incident happens outside of the classroom and a staff person other than the teacher applies consequences, it will be important for that staff person to communicate these measures to the appropriate teachers. That way, if a pattern of bullying is occurring, they can be aware of it.

In some schools, a person other than the classroom teacher is responsible for enforcing discipline. This person often is a school counselor or an individual whose job includes dealing with discipline issues, such as an administrator or a discipline supervisor. If this person is asked to be responsible for following through on bullying issues, he or she will need to rely on a consistent mechanism for reporting incidents, planned consequences, and follow-up strategies to the classroom teacher or other staff member who is closest to the student so that he or she can closely monitor the student's behavior.

• • •

9

Refining Your School's Supervisory System

WHAT YOU WILL LEARN IN CHAPTER 9	
	• how to refine the supervisory system in your school • ways to provide supervision in school "hot spots," such as the playground/athletic fields, lunchroom, restrooms, and classroom • how to evaluate your school's physical design and schedule to find ways to reduce bullying • ways to track and report bullying incidents schoolwide

One of the most important tasks of your school's Bullying Prevention Coordinating Committee will be to review and refine your school's supervisory system, so that bullying is less likely to happen. An important goal will be to use staff in effective ways to monitor and enforce anti-bullying rules throughout your school, and especially in "hot spots" like the playground/athletic fields, restrooms, and lunchroom.

The more staff members are engaged in this supervision, the more bullying will be seen and addressed, and the less likely bullying will continue. This is what is called a supervisory system. Most likely your school already has a supervisory system in place. Reviewing and refining this supervisory system to specifically address bullying is another key component of *OBPP*.

What Are the "Hot Spots" for Bullying in Your School?

You can determine where the "hot spots" are in your school by looking at the results of your Olweus Bullying Questionnaire. These data will provide a picture of the prevalence, nature, and common locations of bullying incidents in your school. You can use this information to refine your supervisory system.

Typically a school's hot spots for bullying will include areas where adult-child ratios are poor, areas where there is less structure, areas where there are many students in one area, and locations that are staffed by school personnel who are perceived by students to have less authority. Such locations include the playground/athletic fields, locker rooms, the lunchroom, and buses.

Areas where students are out of direct view of adults can also be trouble spots; these include restrooms, coatrooms, beneath staircases, hallways that have no classrooms, and places out of view on school grounds. However, a significant number of students report that they are bullied in their classroom. Your BPCC will want to examine your school's questionnaire data to determine the most effective way to address problems in these hot spots.

Although attention may be focused primarily on hot spots, don't forget that bullying may occur in all areas of the school, though less frequently. Until program systems are in place, you may also notice that bullying may "travel" from one location to the next, as students notice more adult supervision in particular hot spots.

In addition, since older students often bully younger students, you may want to consider keeping these groups separate or minimizing contact during transitions, recess, or lunch. Your BPCC might also want to consider ways of building positive collaborations between older and younger students as a means of providing a protective factor for younger students during higher-risk activities (for example, cross-grade "buddies" for reading, a buddy system when riding the bus, or older student mentors who can lead activities at recess).

How Much Supervision Is Enough?

Research has shown that when there are more adults to supervise students, particularly during breaks, fewer bullying problems occur.[1] It is not possible to recommend a specific number of supervising adults (per 100 students, for example) during recess/breaks. To some extent, this will depend on such factors as

- the size and layout of your school playground/athletic fields
- how recess/breaks are organized in your school
- your staff's attitudes and behavior
- staff training and their power and effectiveness to intervene
- school policies about who can and should intervene

If, for example, all of the students are out for recess at the same time and the school grounds have many "hiding places," this will obviously require a greater "adult density" than if the layout is more easily watched or adults are stationed in greater proximity to students.

The goal is to have an adequate number of adults among the students so there is good supervision of what students are doing. The likelihood of discovering bullying and other negative behavior during recess/breaks (and otherwise) should then be high.

What Is the Role and Attitude of Supervising Adults?

A supervisory system is not just a matter of having enough staff supervising your school's hot spots; the attitudes and behaviors of the supervising adults are of utmost importance. A staff member who does not intervene in a bullying situation communicates to the students that bullying is okay and will not lead to any consequences for the perpetrators. It also serves to reduce bystander empathy for students who are bullied and decreases the likelihood that they will respond to assist and follow school rules.

On the other hand, when supervising adults intervene firmly and consistently, this sends an important signal to the bullying students and possible bystanders: We don't accept bullying in our school and such behavior will be stopped and/or negative consequences will be given.

When adults do intervene, the student who is being bullied or the one who is bullying may claim that their interaction was "just for fun" or otherwise deny or minimize their behaviors. To make matters more difficult, students who are bullied might not contradict this assessment due to embarrassment or fear of retaliation.

Adults need to be able to assess situations to determine if it is rough-and-tumble play, real fighting, or bullying (a chart describing the differences between these three behaviors is provided on the Teacher Guide CD-ROM). They need to carefully observe the students involved in potential bullying situations and step in to provide protection and consequences as needed.

Be sure to discuss the differences between rough-and-tumble play, real fighting, and bullying during your staff trainings, so everyone recognizes the differences and knows how to respond. Encourage staff to follow the guiding principle that it is better to err on the side of intervening too often than not enough.

When students see that aggressive behavior is not accepted and could result in negative consequences, they are less likely to join in. Adult intervention shows that the adults care about, support, and protect the student who is being bullied, which will help to ensure that he or she feels safe from future bullying incidents or retaliation. When adults involve bystanders in this process, they are helping to strengthen the school community.

How Can Adults Use the Rules and Other *OBPP* Components When They Intervene?

It is important to post the four anti-bullying rules in all areas of your school so adults can refer to them easily, whenever and wherever they see bullying happening. A reproducible poster of the four anti-bullying rules is available in English and Spanish on the Schoolwide Guide CD-ROM. Color and black-and-white PDF files are provided of both posters. However, you may want to involve students in activities to design their own posters (see pages 75 and 76). Be sure to also post the rules on the playground and in the lunchroom, restrooms, hallways, buses, and all classrooms.

SP 21

Table tents are also included on the Schoolwide Guide CD-ROM in English and Spanish. These table tents display the four anti-bullying rules and should be set out on lunchroom tables, school library tables, and so on. The table tents are available in both color and black and white.

SP 22

It will also be important for all staff to follow the same procedures when addressing bullying. Intervention procedures are briefly described in chapter 10 of this guide and in more detail in chapter 8 of the Teacher Guide.

What Is a Coordinated Supervisory System?

Your school's supervisory system should be coordinated so that all staff consistently react to bullying and take similar measures when faced with negative behavior. All staff and your BPCC should have thorough discussions about what behaviors call for intervention and how that intervention will take place.

A good forum for these discussions is your staff training day and staff discussion groups. The goal is to have each staff person deal with bullying incidents in a reasonable, consistent manner, from one day or week to the next, as well as in relation to other staff at your school.

Another important part of a coordinated supervisory system is the exchange of information about bullying incidents at your school. Staff who observe bullying

There are a lot of teachers supervising the hallways and the outdoor commons area. Our school staff really does care about their students.

— A MIDDLE SCHOOL STUDENT

or other undesirable behavior should, in addition to intervening, report their observations and any reactions or measures taken to the students' primary classroom teacher or, in the case of middle school/junior high school, the adult who has the strongest relationship with the students (for example, homeroom teacher, school counselor, advisor, or lead teacher). The same procedures should be followed when observing students who often spend recess/breaks completely alone and who appear to be socially isolated.

Your school's BPCC may want to develop a consistent and user-friendly schoolwide method of logging bullying incidents or observations about students at risk for bullying or being bullied. Such a log will reveal patterns and connections in students' behavior or situations that might be easily overlooked. In addition, these logs can be extremely useful in preparing to meet with parents to discuss individual students' involvement in bullying and for monitoring the effectiveness of intervention strategies used.

A sample log or documentation form is available on the Schoolwide Guide CD-ROM. You may want to have staff fill out this form and submit it to your main office or discipline supervisor. 23

How Can You Successfully Supervise the Most Common Hot Spots?

You will want to carefully review findings from your Olweus Bullying Questionnaire to learn where bullying is most likely to occur at your school. However, as was mentioned previously, the most common hot spots in a school tend to be the playground/athletic fields, hallways, lunchrooms, restrooms, and the classroom. Here are some guidelines for handling each of these areas. These suggestions are by no means exhaustive, but they may be a good place to start in discussing additional solutions with your staff.

What Actions Should Be Taken to Supervise the Playground?

Since playgrounds are usually found at elementary schools, this area is of most concern for younger students. In designing a plan to reduce bullying and other antisocial behavior during recess, the first step should be a thorough review of how your playground is designed and how it "functions" for your students. Be sure to involve the students in these discussions (perhaps as a topic of a class meeting) because they can provide valuable information and insights. It is important to consider the following:

- How well arranged is your playground area? Are there hidden places on the playground or around the school grounds where bullying can easily take place without being discovered by adults? Do you have adequate supervision of these places, if they exist?

- Are there patterns to how students use these areas (that is, are certain areas dominated by boys or girls or students at a certain grade level)?
- How are the school grounds used when the students are outside? Are there opportunities for activities that the students will find fun and interesting? Is there room for all of the students, or are there certain groups (for example, older boys with ball games) who largely dominate the available area? If there is not much space for certain groups or activities, would it be sensible to divide the area up into "designated" zones? Or would it be possible to have various groups of students (in different grades) take recess or breaks at different times?
- How does the playground function in different seasons and under various weather conditions? And what is recess like when the students stay inside the school building because of bad weather? Do the students have meaningful things to do at these times?
- Is the playground well equipped and does it have an attractive outdoor environment that encourages positive activities? Even though it has not been documented by research, if students are bored, there is likely to be more bullying. This might be one way that they create more activity or excitement. It is often possible to make the outdoor area more interesting and stimulating with relatively simple and inexpensive measures. Again, it is important that students be allowed to participate in meaningful ways in these decisions.
- Who is doing the supervision? Teachers? Playground supervisors? Do they know the children well? Have they been trained to recognize bullying and intervene appropriately when they observe or suspect it?
- How are adults supervising the playground? Do they huddle together, or do they spread out around the playground where they can observe all areas?

I really think our recess is more fun and better now because I used to get glares and dirty looks—and all that has stopped. Thank you!

— AN ELEMENTARY STUDENT

The way in which the playground is laid out, how recess is organized, and the quality of supervision can be very important both for the students' sense of well-being and the possibilities of preventing and reducing bullying at school. Although the answers to the questions on the previous page might seem obvious, taking steps to make the playground a safer place may make a big difference in your school climate.

What Actions Should Be Taken to Supervise Your School's Hallways?

It will be important to provide adequate supervision of your school's hallways before and after school and during the time when students are moving between classes (if you are in a middle school/junior high school). Here are some suggestions:

- Require that all classroom teachers stand in the hallway while students are moving from class to class and for a certain amount of time before and after school.
- Structure passing times, bus lineup, or large-group activities to reduce the numbers of students present at any given time.
- Consider restructuring student access to hallways to reduce the opportunities to be out of adult sight. Close or restrict access to hidden areas of your school, such as hallways with no classrooms or areas beneath staircases.
- Empower all staff to intervene in bullying incidents that occur in the hallways or other public places. For example, there may be situations where custodial staff or lunchroom staff should intervene on the spot to stop bullying that they observe. These individuals need training and the support of administrators and other staff to do this.
- Have staff locate themselves in those places in your school's hallways where bullying problems have been identified. For example, staff might stand near a particular restroom or certain staircases while students move between classes.
- Consider varying your class schedule so not all students are in the hallways at the same time.

What Actions Should Be Taken to Supervise Your School's Lunchroom?

It will be important to provide adequate supervision of your school's lunchroom. Here are some suggestions:

- Hire lunchroom monitors to supervise this area during mealtimes. Empower these individuals by giving them proper training and authority to intervene in bullying instances where appropriate.

- Ask staff to take turns supervising the lunchroom.
- Have different grade levels eat at different times; in particular, make sure older students don't eat at the same time as younger students.
- Set up lunchroom tables, so there are no blind spots between the students and supervising adults.
- Make sure that all students (especially isolated students) have someone to sit with.
- Stagger lunch times, so students are eating in smaller groups.
- Periodically structure lunch times so that students don't always sit in the same spots. Eat in a different setting ("picnic outside" or create classroom "dining rooms") or provide students with an icebreaker question or activity that encourages them to find out something new about people at their table. This strategy can be particularly useful with secondary-level students.
- Require that lunch times have a civil tone. Often, lunch times are loud and chaotic—and adults may even use whistles or bullhorns as management strategies. This is not conducive to healthy digestion, let alone good behavior.

Younger students can be coached to use good manners. Surprise students occasionally by providing "props" for fine dining: students or parent-teacher organizations might design or contribute tablecloths, flowers or centerpieces, or quiet music to create a more relaxed and civil atmosphere.

What Actions Should Be Taken to Supervise Student Restrooms?

Here are some suggestions for handling student restrooms:

- Have adults stand just outside the restrooms and make periodic visits inside the restrooms for a time before and after school and while students are moving from class to class.
- Don't allow students to use restrooms that are in out-of-the-way places. Prevent their use by locking the doors.
- Require students to ask for a pass to go to the restroom and don't allow more than one student to go at a time.

What Actions May Be Taken to Supervise Students on the Bus or on the Way to and from School?

- Post the four anti-bullying rules on buses.
- Provide *OBPP* training for all bus drivers.
- Recruit volunteers to monitor the bus stops and provide training regarding how to intervene and report on bullying.

- Involve crossing guards and school resource officers in bullying prevention training and request their assistance in monitoring the behavior of students who walk to school.
- Be aware of hot spots along common walking routes and recruit/train volunteers to act as "safety patrol" to monitor and assist students at risk in these areas.
- Arrange for students at risk of being bullied to have a group of "walking buddies" or "bus buddies" who can provide social support and act as buffers against bullying.
- Brainstorm ways to provide additional supervision for individuals or groups of students who are prone to bully other students.
- Provide rules, staff monitors, and activities if students congregate outside of school before or after school.

What Actions Should Be Taken to Supervise Students in the Classroom?
Pages 63–65 in the Teacher Guide detail how classroom teachers should set up their classrooms to prevent and reduce bullying. It will be helpful for your BPCC to read through this section of the Teacher Guide as they plan their schoolwide supervisory system.

What Can You Do about Your School's Physical Design That Will Help Reduce or Prevent Bullying?

Depending on what you learn from your Olweus Bullying Questionnaire about bullying "hot spots," you may want to make changes to the physical design of your school. Here are just a few examples:

- Close off hidden areas of your school, such as hallways with no classrooms or areas beneath staircases, or install mirrors to allow all areas to be readily supervised.
- As mentioned earlier, lock the doors of out-of-the-way restrooms, so students can't use them.
- Remove physical barriers on the playground, such as bushes or privacy fences that allow children to be hidden from view.

As you can see, bullying prevention is not just about educating your students. It also requires educating adults about their role in bullying prevention and how to carry out this role. Although some educators and other staff may not want this responsibility, it is essential that all staff see themselves as supervisors whenever they are in the presence of students. It is also about structuring your school's physical environment so there is less opportunity for bullying to happen.

Now, let's look at the procedures staff should use in intervening in bullying situations.

• • •

10

Dealing with Bullying on the Individual Level

WHAT YOU WILL LEARN IN CHAPTER 10	
	• how to intervene on the spot in bullying situations • strategies to talk with students who bully and students who are bullied • how to approach parents of students who bully and students who are bullied • what to do if you suspect bullying might be going on and need to investigate further

It is very important that school staff take action as soon as they suspect or have been informed of a bullying problem. Unfortunately, adults don't always intervene. Sometimes it is because they have trouble recognizing bullying. Some adults don't intervene because they don't see bullying as an important issue. Finally, some adults don't intervene because they are not sure what to do.

This chapter provides a brief overview of intervention procedures. A more detailed description is provided in chapter 8 of the Teacher Guide. It will be very important, as leaders of your schoolwide effort, to make sure all staff are trained in how to use these intervention procedures and are continually encouraged and supported in using them effectively. Staff trainings and regular staff discussion groups both provide good forums for practicing these interventions.

Note: If your school has a staff person who is responsible for following through on discipline issues, your BPCC will need to establish clear procedures regarding when and how bullying incidents should be handled by this person or by the teacher or staff member who has the closest relationship to the students involved. Whenever possible, we encourage the involvement of those who have a more personal relationship and daily contact with students.

What Should Staff Do When They See Bullying Happen?

Let's start with situations where staff observe bullying happening or need to break up a bullying incident on the spot. All adults in your school (including bus drivers, custodians, nurses, hall monitors, playground supervisors, office support staff, classroom teachers, and substitute teachers) should be trained and empowered to take the following steps to intervene, protect the student who is being bullied, and empower the bystanders:

Step 1: Stop the bullying.

Step 2: Support the student who has been bullied.

Step 3: To the bullying student(s): Name the bullying behavior and refer to the four anti-bullying rules.

Step 4: Empower the bystanders with appreciation if they were supportive to the student who was bullied or with information about how to act in the future.

Step 5: Impose immediate and appropriate consequences for the student(s) who bullied.

Step 6: Take steps to make sure the bullied student will be protected from future bullying.

Note: A reproducible tip sheet with these six steps is provided on the Schoolwide Guide CD-ROM. Make copies, laminate them, and have staff carry a copy with them for easy reference on how to respond in bullying situations.

A more detailed description of what to do (and not do) in each step and information on how to effectively use verbal reprimands is also available on the Schoolwide CD-ROM.

The one thing I like best about *OBPP* is that it teaches school staff to really concentrate on the student who was bullied first and then deal with the students who are bullying.

— PREVENTION SPECIALIST

What Type of Follow-Up Should You Do after the Immediate Intervention?

After their initial intervention in a bullying incident, staff will need to report the bullying to the students' primary teacher(s) or the staff member who has the closest relationship to each student, and possibly to school administrators or your school's discipline supervisor. Your BPCC should set up procedures for this reporting.

In many cases, follow-up discussions will be required with the students involved in the bullying incident. Staff will want to have separate follow-up meetings with the student who was bullied and with the student(s) who bullied. Just note that not all staff do these kinds of follow-up meetings with students. In some schools administrators or counselors do this work. Where possible, it is recommended that this follow-up meeting be done by the primary teacher or staff person who has the most positive relationship with each student.

Not every bullying incident will require a follow-up meeting. The extent or severity of the bullying and the likely impact it is having on the bullied student should be considered when deciding whether a follow-up meeting is called for. The amount of reliable information staff has about an incident and the bullying relationships between the students involved is another important factor. When in doubt, staff should err on the side of holding meetings. This follow-up meeting should be done as soon after the bullying incident as possible.

Your BPCC will want to provide guidance on what situations require follow-up, what form that follow-up should take, who should be responsible, and how the effectiveness of the follow-up intervention will be monitored.

What Should Staff Do When They Are Told about a Possible Bullying Problem Involving One of Their Students?

Sometimes staff may become aware of a possible bullying problem, perhaps through reports from classmates of a bullied student. Or perhaps the bullied student has contacted the staff person about the difficult situation.

If staff feel uncertain about the accuracy of the reports received, there are several strategies they can use to find out more information (discussed on pages 103–106 in the Teacher Guide). As a general guideline, staff should always take reports of bullying very seriously and assume that they are largely correct.

The first step in making sure the information is accurate is for the staff member to meet with the student who has been reported to be bullied and his or her parents. The staff member may choose to meet first with the student only and then with the parents, or he or she may schedule a meeting with both the student and parents together. The purpose of this meeting is to determine/acknowledge what happened, offer support, and provide assurance about the staff person's commitment to getting the bullying to stop.

Once the staff person has had a conversation with the student who is being bullied and his or her parent(s), the staff member will need to directly confront the bullying student or students. The staff member should do this as quickly as possible after having identified the student(s) involved and gleaned the necessary information.

It may also be helpful to have another adult (such as another teacher, counselor, assistant principal, or school resource officer) included in this conversation with the bullying student or group of students, especially if one or more of them could be difficult to handle. Having another adult present sends the message that this is a serious situation. One adult should lead the conversation, however.

If more than one student was involved in the bullying, staff should not talk to the bullying students together as a group, but should talk to each one individually and right after one another in quick succession so they have little opportunity to share what was discussed. It is likely that one student played a "leader" role in the bullying. Staff should talk to this student first, if they know who it is.

At this meeting, the staff member should set consequences and be clear about his or her expectations that the behavior will stop. It is advised that the parents of the student or students be told about or involved in these meetings as well.

Staff should check back with all students involved, individually, in two to three days to see whether the bullying has stopped and to offer additional support or needed interventions. Finally, staff should communicate with other staff members who may need to be informed about these events.

A meeting outline and script for having follow-up meetings with both the student who is bullied and the student who is bullying others are provided on the Teacher Guide CD-ROM.

How Should You Address Student Bullying with Parents?

Note: The term "parents" is used here, but it refers to parents, guardians, or other family caregivers who have primary responsibility for the well-being of the student involved.

A brief overview of how to work with parents in addressing bullying problems at school will be covered here. The Teacher Guide details how to involve parents of students who are bullied, students who bully, and students who are bystanders in bullying situations. See pages 94–97 and 100–102 in the Teacher Guide for more information.

Your BPCC will need to determine when it will be appropriate and who should be responsible for contacting parents to talk about bullying that their child may be experiencing (or participating in). In some schools, classroom teachers take on this task. In other schools, the school counselor or the principal typically makes these contacts. In still other schools, students who have bullied others are required to call their parents (under the guidance of an adult) to initiate a discussion about their behavior.

Whenever possible, we encourage the staff person with the closest relationship with the student (typically the primary teacher or advisor) to make this call, due to the personal relationship they will have with the parents. The person making the call should have good rapport with the parents and the patience to work through difficult, emotional situations with them. Your BPCC will be responsible for creating your school's procedural guidelines on this issue.

Also be sure your school has an open-door policy with parents regarding this issue. Encourage parent meetings (both at the schoolwide level and classroom level) to discuss the role parents can play in bullying prevention, what staff are doing to address it, information about school policies and procedures, and procedures for parents to share information/report bullying to school staff.

It can be particularly difficult to approach the parents of students who are bullying others. Often these parents are not ready to hear that their child is causing harm to others. For some, this may be the first time they have received this message. They may be more supportive of your school's efforts if they (and all parents) have previously received information about bullying, your school's rules and consequences for bullying, and the procedures for notifying parents of bullying problems. (See chapter 13 of this guide and chapter 9 of the Teacher Guide for more information about involving parents as partners in the program.)

You will also want to address bystander behavior with parents. See the Teacher Guide, page 102, for suggestions about working with these parents. Both English and Spanish tip sheets for parents to address the bullying issue at home are also provided on the Teacher Guide CD-ROM. Handouts should never replace personal conversations with parents; rather, they are intended to supplement these discussions.

These are some of the important steps your staff can take in intervening in bullying situations. Again, for more detailed procedures, read chapter 8 in the Teacher Guide.

• • •

11

Introducing the Program to Students

WHAT YOU WILL LEARN IN CHAPTER 11	• how to set up and implement a schoolwide *OBPP* kick-off event • how to implement other schoolwide efforts to promote *OBPP* with students

A special event is a good way to introduce *OBPP* to all your students at one time. Schools have approached a "kick-off" event in many exciting ways with various themes. Some involve parents and community members as well as students; some hold a series of events (each tailored to a different group) held over the period of a few days or a week. In the midst of the celebration, don't forget that there are serious messages that need to be conveyed as well.

When Should the Kick-Off Event Take Place?

The kick-off event should take place after all administrators, teachers, and other staff are trained in *OBPP,* and after all plans are in place to implement the program in your school. You may want to wait until you have the results of your administration of the Olweus Bullying Questionnaire, so highlights of this information can be presented to everyone who attends.

Ideally, the kick-off should come at a logical "beginning point" in the school calendar, such as near the beginning of the school year or just after winter break. School personnel should carefully consider the timeline for the program (see pages 13–14) before setting the date for the school kick-off event, so you are sure that all tasks leading up to the launch have been completed first. If you are not able to hold a schoolwide kick-off event, consider having separate grade-level kick-off events instead.

After the initial program launch, make plans to hold a kick-off event at the beginning of every school year to re-energize students and staff and to remind everyone that bullying will continue to be addressed.

What Steps Should Your School Take to Prepare and Present This Kick-Off Event?

Members of the BPCC should plan the kick-off event and actively participate in it as well. BPCC members should be introduced during the event, so all students and staff know who they are. The program should include brief statements, skits, or other presentations by school personnel (such as members of your BPCC) or students.

Participating students might be members of a student advisory group to *OBPP* (if there is one), members of a drama club, or participants in other student organizations that work toward improved student relationships. They can be positive role models for the other students.

You could invite parents to this event, or you could have a separate school-
SP 27 wide parent meeting (discussed in chapter 13). A sample invitation that can be
sent out to parents or community members is provided on the Schoolwide Guide
CD-ROM in English and Spanish. Also available on the CD-ROM are some
28 announcements that can be read over your school's public address system as a
way to promote the kick-off event to your students.

It is important that as many members of the school community as possible—including teachers, administrators, after-school program staff, and playground and lunchroom monitors—attend this event to show parents and students their support and enthusiasm for the program.

Planning for this event should happen several weeks before the program is scheduled to begin at your school. The BPCC workbook has activities that will help guide this planning. Teachers will want to be prepared to facilitate their first class meetings shortly after this kick-off event as well.

What Should Be Covered in the Kick-Off Event?

The kick-off event should be creative, be energizing, be informative, and generally include the following elements:

- Introduce the BPCC. Committee members should be introduced during the event so all students and staff know who they are.
- Present the four anti-bullying rules. Schools have been quite creative in how they introduce school rules, using student or adult skits; chants, cheers, or

"raps"; and posters or banners to spell out and demonstrate the four anti-bullying rules.

- Present some basic information about bullying and *OBPP* in your school.

A sample outline for a kick-off event with the related key messages that should be covered is available on the Schoolwide Guide CD-ROM. 29 Be sure to make this event as creative and fun as possible, without losing the opportunity to convey these important messages to your student body.

What Additional Activities Could You Do as Part of the Kick-Off to Your Program?

Your BPCC may wish to develop other schoolwide activities that help kick off *OBPP* in your school. Here are some ideas that other schools have used for their kick-off events:

- Post the *OBPP* anti-bullying rules poster (see page 60) throughout your school. *Note:* Posting the rules is not optional, but using these posters is.
- Make stickers with anti-bullying themes. Hand these out at the kick-off event or other *OBPP* events.
- Have teachers or students perform skits for different classrooms. Then follow up with a discussion among students. Perhaps a pretaped version could be shown by each classroom teacher and discussed at a class meeting. Here are some skit ideas:
    a. Acting out what each rule means and how students can follow the rules in bullying situations
    b. Demonstrating the different roles in the Bullying Circle
    c. Modeling ways to include students who are left out
- Create an "infomercial" to introduce the program. This can be performed in each classroom by staff or a select group of students, or it can be performed over your school's public address system or television channel. Sample infomercials or announcements are available on the Schoolwide Guide CD-ROM (see page 74).
- Host a rap contest. Students write and perform anti-bullying raps for prizes.
- Host a logo, slogan, motto, or poster contest with anti-bullying themes. The winning entry could be used to create a promotional item (see next idea). Sample slogans include "Our school is united against bullying!" or "Care! Share! Be aware! Help stop bullying in our school."

- Create a banner/flag/T-shirt/button/book cover to promote the program. Have classes come up with ideas and award a pizza party to the winning students' class. Invite community businesses to sponsor the cost of these items. Have teachers wear the T-shirts or buttons on the day their first class meetings are held. Promotional items, such as T-shirts or pencils, could also be awarded to students for positive, prosocial behavior.
- Conduct parent events. Use existing opportunities, such as back-to-school night or parent-teacher conferences, to share information about *OBPP* with parents; send home a newsletter and/or packet of program information to parents. Host a dinner night for families to introduce the program or set up a special table of bullying prevention information at parent-teacher conferences.
- Work with older students (for example, a middle school or high school drama club or social action club) to give presentations with anti-bullying messages to students in an assembly or in individual classrooms. Prior to the event, make sure the actors are well prepared and that the skits are appropriate. Also ensure that adequate time is set aside following the skits to allow students to discuss appropriate resolutions to bullying.
- Develop a schoolwide bulletin board, Web page, or newsletter with anti-bullying messages. Use these tools to update the school community on your program's progress.
- Host a cooperative game day to develop student team-building.
- Invite guest speakers, area performers who offer creative assemblies or other programming related to the topic, or local sports figures to speak to your students and parents about bullying. Carefully screen these individuals first to make sure their messages are in line with *OBPP* goals and principles. Make sure that local celebrities have positive reputations free of bullying!

What Should Happen after the Kick-Off Event?

The first class meetings should happen shortly after the kick-off event (ideally later that same day). These meetings should begin with a discussion of what class meetings are, the four anti-bullying rules, what they mean, and what behaviors are considered bullying. How to support these classroom efforts will be discussed further in the next chapter.

• • •

12

Supporting the Program in the Classroom

WHAT YOU WILL LEARN IN CHAPTER 12	
	• the steps that need to be taken to implement class meetings effectively • ways that your school leadership can support the use of class meetings

Shortly after the schoolwide kick-off event, teachers should begin conducting weekly class meetings. Class meetings are a key component of *OBPP.*

RESEARCH FACT

> An *OBPP* research study has shown that teachers who systematically used class meetings in their anti-bullying work obtained larger reductions in bullying problems one year after introduction of *OBPP* compared to those who used class meetings to a lesser degree or not at all.[1]

Note: Many teachers may already use class meetings as part of their classroom routine or as part of another program. To implement *OBPP,* these teachers can maintain the structure of their class meetings but focus their discussions on bullying and related issues.

What Steps Should Be Taken to Organize and Lead Class Meetings?

Class meetings should be held regularly, preferably at least once a week. For upper primary and middle or junior high students, the meetings could last 30 to 40 minutes. Meetings for younger students could last 15 to 30 minutes. With younger students teachers may also want to have more than one meeting per week.

It is important to remember that class meetings are not the same as curriculum lessons. The teacher's role in leading class meetings is more of a facilitator than teacher. This does not mean he or she will not guide the discussion. The teacher will need to make sure his or her discussion goals are met through careful probing and open-ended questioning. Class meetings are an opportunity for students to share their feelings and opinions, and to suggest solutions, as they learn to follow the rules and handle bullying situations appropriately. Class meeting outlines and scripts are available on the Teacher Guide CD-ROM.

It is helpful for teachers to realize that although their class meetings for *OBPP* will initially focus on the topic of bullying, these meetings can be used for other topics as well. Students may become bored if bullying is the only topic discussed. Class meetings can be viewed as a forum to discuss any issues that come up at school, to build class cohesiveness and community, and to recognize achievements and successes of the class as a whole. For other class meeting topic ideas see pages 74–75 in the Teacher Guide.

Teachers will vary in their experience and comfort level with class meetings. There is no one right way to lead a class meeting. Some teachers prefer to have a very clear idea of what is going to be discussed, so sample scripts are provided on the Teacher Guide CD-ROM. Other teachers desire a more open-ended style that provides flexibility to discuss issues as they come up. Either approach is fine.

If teachers don't feel comfortable leading these meetings at first, they are encouraged to ask for help from the BPCC. Perhaps one of the BPCC members could lead (or co-lead) the first couple of meetings for this teacher. Or the teacher could consider asking another teacher with experience in class meetings to co-facilitate. Your BPCC may also decide to offer additional training on conducting class meetings, or teachers may raise issues about these meetings at staff discussion groups.

For more information on organizing and implementing class meetings, see pages 69–72 in the Teacher Guide.

What Can Your Schoolwide Leadership Team Do to Support These Classroom Efforts?

There are a number of things your school administration and BPCC can do to support the program efforts that are going on in the classroom.

- The BPCC should monitor teacher progress with class meetings through record-keeping and communication with teachers so that support, mentoring, materials, and training can be provided to maximize their success. A Class Meeting Activity Log is provided on the Teacher Guide CD-ROM. Your BPCC may want teachers to fill this out and turn it in periodically.

Because the BPCC has an overarching view of the program, this group will have a key role in ensuring that class meeting topics and approaches vary both within a grade and across grades.

- School administrators can make it clear to teachers that they have permission to take time to hold their class meetings and stress the importance of doing so.
- The administration should recognize the extra time and effort it will take to prepare for and hold these meetings so teachers feel supported and appreciated.
- The school administration and the BPCC should work together to determine the best way to schedule class meetings in your school. They will need to decide, for example, whether there should be a set time or day that all classrooms will hold these meetings, or whether this should be left to the discretion of teachers. In some cases, administrators may need to work to slightly rearrange weekly schedules or designate a particular time (for example, a student activity period once a week) to allow time for class meetings.
- As mentioned earlier, support systems should be put into place to assist teachers who feel uncomfortable leading class meetings.
- If some teachers refuse to hold class meetings, the administration needs to clearly communicate that they are expected to participate in this schoolwide program. They should be aware that the students in their classrooms are being deprived of very important information and an experience that students in other classrooms are receiving.
- The BPCC should anticipate and proactively address teachers' potential concerns about implementing class meetings (such as lack of time, concern about the lack of academic content, lack of time for preparation, or viewing bullying prevention as a low priority).

The BPCC can highlight the benefits of the program and can work with your school's administration to facilitate solutions to some of the teachers'

Class meetings have really helped with outside recess. Kids are really following the rules and treating each other with more respect.

— AN ELEMENTARY STUDENT

concerns. Sharing information from teachers who have successfully implemented *OBPP* class meetings and hearing how they save time by reducing discipline problems is also useful.

- School administrators can express their support of using academic time for class meetings because many of the activities that students will be doing in the meetings require critical thinking and problem-solving skills that can be transferred to other subject areas.
- The BPCC and teachers should work collaboratively to identify ways to extend bullying prevention concepts across the curriculum and to make connections with academic themes and activities in other subjects, such as math, language arts, social studies, health, and the arts (for more ideas on this, see the Teacher Guide CD-ROM).

Addressing teachers' concerns and showing them how class meetings will help them achieve their academic goals for students often reduces their resistance to holding class meetings.

Why Is It Important to Provide Adequate Training for Classroom Teachers?

In order for teachers to feel confident leading class meetings, they need to be well trained and have a clear understanding of the problem of bullying. Besides your initial full-day staff training, you may want to provide additional training for your classroom teachers, specifically focused on holding class meetings and using role-plays. You could also use this training event as an opportunity to address other classroom issues in program implementation. This additional training could be conducted by a BPCC member or members, or contracted with your school's certified Olweus trainer.

We have our class meetings every Thursday, and they are fun.
It has changed our school quite a bit.

— A MIDDLE SCHOOL STUDENT

Kids love to share stories, and class meetings give them the opportunity to share while conveying an anti-bullying message.

— PREVENTION SPECIALIST

What Additional Resources Are Available on Class Meetings?

A variety of supplemental materials (such as children's literature and audio-visual aids) are available to support class meetings. Your certified Olweus trainer can suggest grade-appropriate supplemental classroom curricula as well as student literature and materials that are aligned with the program goals and principles. (There is also a list of recommended resources on the Teacher Guide CD-ROM.)

A variety of print and Internet resources are also available on the subject of class meetings. Check with your certified Olweus trainer, school librarian, or local community library for these resources.

The key to class meetings is to hold them consistently and to organize them in such a way that students feel the meetings are their meetings. Teachers should focus on creating a safe environment where students feel they can openly share ideas and opinions. This effort will pay big dividends in addressing bullying and a variety of other issues among your students.

• • •

13

Partnering with Parents

WHAT YOU WILL LEARN IN CHAPTER 13	
	• how to involve parents in schoolwide and classroom bullying prevention strategies • how to support classroom-level parent meetings • how to develop stronger partnerships with parents

Note: As in the last chapter, the term "parents" is used here, but it refers to parents, guardians, or other family caregivers who have primary responsibility for the well-being of the student involved.

■

Parent involvement is helpful and even essential for the smooth running of many aspects of school life. It is also an important component of *OBPP.*

Note: Please keep in mind that this discussion will be describing ideal parent participation, with an understanding that involving parents is often easier said than done. Because families experience numerous demands on scarce time, nearly all schools struggle with finding optimal ways to reach parents and to maximize their involvement.

Why Should Staff Involve Parents in *OBPP?*

Now that your school has decided to implement *OBPP,* positive parent-staff relationships are even more important. Here are some reasons why:

- Parents can reinforce the same anti-bullying messages and social rules about caring for others at home. This provides a consistent message for students in all areas of their lives.
- It will be much easier to talk with parents about a bullying problem if you have already established a positive relationship with them.

- Students will be taught to tell an adult if they or someone else is being bullied, and adults (including adults at home) must understand the best ways to intervene.
- Staff will have an opportunity to explain to parents how the program will work in your school and in the classroom.
- Staff can point parents to resources and strategies that they can use to help prevent and reduce possible bullying problems.
- Actively involving parents can also open the door to getting their help in refining and implementing the program in your school, by serving on the BPCC and by helping in individual classrooms.
- Staff will have the opportunity to invite parents to schoolwide and class meetings.

How Can You Involve Parents and Family Members in Your School's Implementation of *OBPP?*

Usually, the first step in promoting parent involvement in *OBPP* efforts is selecting a key parent (or parents) to serve as members of the BPCC. It is very important that at least one parent sit on this committee to support bullying prevention efforts. It is best to choose a parent who is energetic, organized, and comfortable speaking with other parents.

In addition to serving on your school's BPCC, parents can also be involved in *OBPP* in the following ways:

- Help organize classroom parent meetings. Parents can be asked to help organize classroom parent meetings by providing food or calling other parents to remind them to attend.
- Attend the schoolwide parent meeting. You are encouraged to have a schoolwide kick-off meeting/event that will give parents an introduction to the program, help them understand the need for the program, and identify how they can help at school and at home. You may want to encourage your classroom teachers to offer classroom-level parent meetings immediately after this schoolwide parent meeting.
- Attend classroom parent meetings. Ideally, teachers should hold two to three meetings with parents of students in their class over the course of the school year, depending on their schedules and the availability of parents. More information on how to run these meetings is provided in the Teacher Guide (chapter 9).

- Talk with their children about bullying. There is a parent pamphlet on the Schoolwide Guide CD-ROM that you can mail to parents or have classroom teachers send home with their students. This pamphlet provides background information about bullying, suggested strategies for discussing bullying with their children, and an overview of the school's program. This pamphlet also stresses the need for parents to intervene in bullying situations when they become aware of them. Both Spanish and English versions are available.

Here are some other ways to keep parents informed and involved in *OBPP:*

- Provide a short orientation about bullying and *OBPP* at a "back-to-school" night or other standing parent meetings.
- Require teachers to call parents during the first few weeks of school to begin establishing a working relationship with them. Making this initial positive contact with parents by phone or in person early in the year lays the groundwork for better communication when staff do have to call parents about a problem or concern with their child.
- Develop parent-child homework assignments that deal with bullying-related topics.
- Talk to parents about *OBPP* during routine parent-teacher conferences.
- Your school may already have a home communication system in place, such as a regular newsletter, notes that are sent home, emails, or a Web page. These strategies are very effective measures to keep parents informed of what is going on in your school and to invite them to communicate with you; you may also use these measures to inform parents of how your school is implementing *OBPP.* If your school does not currently have such systems in place, your BPCC should discuss ways to organize some.

In your efforts to engage parents in your bullying prevention efforts, consider what works and doesn't work for the parents at your school. Here are some issues to consider:

- time of day/work schedules
- transportation needs
- child care needs
- literacy
- languages spoken
- what attracts parents to school events (personal invitations, student invitations, providing practical information for parents, food, student

participation or performances, transportation provided, fun activities, opportunities to meet and socialize with other parents or talk to the teacher, door prizes, and so on)

After initial contact, it is important for staff, particularly the classroom teacher, to keep in touch with parents as much as possible. For more information about how to talk to parents about a specific bullying problem that involves their child, see chapter 8 in the Teacher Guide.

What Should You Do during Your Schoolwide Parent Meeting?

A good way to introduce your bullying prevention effort is to hold a schoolwide parent meeting. You are encouraged to send out an introductory letter informing
SP 31 parents of the program and this meeting. A sample letter is found on the Schoolwide Guide CD-ROM in English and Spanish.

At the schoolwide parent meeting, give parents an overview of the seriousness of the bullying problem in your school (including an overview of data from the Olweus Bullying Questionnaire), what steps your school is taking to address the issue, and the important role they can play (at school and at home) in supporting these efforts.

This parent meeting could be held immediately after your schoolwide kick-off event for students and parents, during a parent open house, or at or after a PTA/PTO meeting.

32 A sample outline for this schoolwide parent meeting is provided on the Schoolwide Guide CD-ROM.

What Will Teachers Be Doing during Their Classroom-Level Parent Meetings?

Teachers of elementary grades are encouraged to hold classroom-level parent meetings, which are designed to help the teacher and parents get to know each other better and feel more comfortable with and connected to each other. This improved communication is likely to lead to a more positive classroom environment. At the middle school/junior high school level, teachers may want to hold team-level or grade-level meetings.

The meetings also provide opportunities for parents to learn more about bullying and related problems and about your school's anti-bullying work through *OBPP*. If teachers don't feel comfortable leading these meetings themselves, they may want to have someone co-lead the meeting with them or hold grade-level parent meetings at first.

As mentioned earlier, it is suggested that teachers hold two to three parent meetings during the school year, if possible. These meetings could be held in conjunction with parent-teacher organizational meetings and/or parent conferences. If teachers are working with older students, it might be a good idea to include them in one of these meetings. Teachers may also want to supplement these meetings with one or two social events that include the students, for example, at the end of each semester. These types of events help build a greater sense of community in the classroom.

Room parents or volunteers can help teachers organize these meetings by

- helping with invitations
- bringing snacks or beverages or asking other parents to do so
- setting up chairs in a circle
- making name tags with both the parent's name and child's name on them
- taking meeting minutes and sending them out to all classroom parents

The Teacher Guide provides an outline for the first classroom-level parent meeting, some ideas for additional parent topics, and tips for running these meetings (see the Teacher Guide, chapter 9).

• • •

14

Developing Community Efforts

WHAT YOU WILL LEARN IN CHAPTER 14	
	• how to engage community support for your program • how to promote your program and anti-bullying messages throughout your community • how to facilitate partnerships with community stakeholders

It is a good idea to engage your larger community in your bullying prevention efforts. Even though the majority of bullying incidents take place on school grounds during school hours, bullying doesn't cease at the doors to your school. It exists at school bus stops, community parks, summer camps, neighborhoods, and anywhere that young people gather. Community members can help spread anti-bullying messages and efforts outside your school as well as provide support and resources to enhance the program within your building.

Ideally, students should receive consistent anti-bullying messages in all areas of their lives. Seeing billboards, posters, or signs of community sponsorship or support for your school's bullying prevention program tells students that bullying is not just a school issue that is important to teachers, but an issue that is important to the whole community.

Strong community support can also help to safeguard your program from possible criticism by parents, community members, politicians, or the media. This disapproval might come from those who don't understand the program's preventive focus and believe that any school that systematically addresses bullying must have serious "bullying problems." Criticism also may come from those who do not understand the long-term nature of *OBPP* and feel the need to criticize short-term outcomes that provide anything less than dramatic reductions in bullying.

What Are Some Ways Community Groups Can Support Bullying Prevention Efforts?

Community groups can provide your bullying prevention program with different types of support, including financial, material, human, and public relations support. Here is a description of each:

Financial Support

For those schools whose bullying prevention efforts are supported by grants or other time-limited funding, begin to think now about how you can sustain your bullying prevention efforts after your current funding has ended.

There are not a lot of long-term expenses in implementing *OBPP,* but you may want funding for replacement Teacher Guides and Schoolwide Guides (as needed), the yearly kick-off events, yearly administration of the Olweus Bullying Questionnaire, stipends for OBPP coordinators or BPCC members, supplemental materials for your school's library or classrooms, rewards for students, community billboards, and so on.

Consider local foundations, businesses, or organizations (for example, Knights of Columbus, Veterans of Foreign Wars, Rotarians, Masons, and Junior League) that you might approach for funding to supplement your school's bullying prevention budget. Also consider your school's own PTO/PTA as a source of financial support. Be concrete in your requests for assistance. Let businesses know specifically how their financial donations will be used, and once the funds are given, be sure to promote the contribution and send a letter of thanks. Here are some ways community groups can support your efforts:

- A local grocery store donates a portion of the day's or week's sales to a school when a special coupon is presented by a store customer.
- The Masons donate a portion of funds raised for anti-violence efforts in the community for an anti-bullying banner to hang in the school cafeteria.
- Rotarians create special billboards and host the school's kick-off event.

Material Support

Some businesses and organizations are more comfortable in providing tangible material support rather than financial support. For example, the owner of a paper mill might agree to purchase materials for teachers as a donation to your school. On a smaller scale, a local pizza restaurant might be glad to donate ten pizzas for a parent kick-off event or an in-school celebration to recognize "random acts of kindness" by students. Or a local copy shop might agree to laminate your anti-bullying posters and banners as their donation to your program.

Human Support

In addition to giving from their pocketbooks, community members can, of course, give of their time. Here are just a few ways that community members can support bullying prevention programs by their presence within a school:

- serve as a member of your BPCC
- volunteer to supervise recess or after-school play times
- report concerns about students bullying others in the community to your school leadership
- assist with the production of a student play with anti-bullying themes
- be a "buddy" or a mentor to students who may feel isolated or who are exhibiting bullying behavior
- join with school personnel, parents, and students in a show of support for the program by attending special events at the school (such as linking hands around the school building)
- offer special services (such as movie passes, store discounts, or coupons) for students who have been "caught" engaging in caring, supportive behaviors

Public Relations Support

Good press can be extremely beneficial for your bullying prevention program and for emphasizing the importance of bullying prevention throughout the community. Identify local newspaper and/or TV stations that have displayed sensitivity to covering educational issues in your community, and invite them to your school to learn more about your program. Provide them with sample materials, a program fact sheet, and so on to help ensure that the press coverage will be thorough, accurate, and positive.

Bad press can be harmful to your efforts. Although most reporters will recognize the importance of bullying prevention, on occasion, published stories may include inaccurate information, may sensationalize particular bullying incidents, or may assume a negative focus or tone. (For example, reporters might assume that if school X launches a bullying prevention program, it must have a serious discipline problem. Others might argue that *OBPP* "coddles" students who are bullied and that these students would fare better if they would just "stick up for themselves.")

As noted above, negative press can usually be avoided by being proactive (for example, soliciting interest from reporters), identifying reporters who have a reputation for handling such issues intelligently and sensitively, preparing well for their visit and/or phone call, and providing them adequate materials that describe the program.

Here are some ways that you can work with the local media to help publicize your school's bullying prevention efforts:

- Write press releases to announce an event or give an update on the progress of the program. These press releases can be sent to TV, radio, or print media. 33 After sending a press release, follow it up with a phone call. If the press release is used, write a note of appreciation. A sample press release is included on the Schoolwide Guide CD-ROM.
- Write a letter to the editor or a reader's opinion column about the effects of bullying or what your school is doing to prevent it. Respond to incidents of bullying in your community or even other parts of the country.
- Hold a news conference to publicize the program and its progress. Show graphs to reflect the program's success or perform skits from your kick-off event. You can set the stage to make these news conferences interesting and eye-catching.

How Can You Spread an Anti-Bullying Message to Your Broader Community?

In addition to engaging community members in support of your school's bullying prevention program, consider looking at ways to spread anti-bullying messages to the broader community. Bullying is not just a school issue; it is a community issue and a public health issue. Information on bullying would be helpful to adults who are associated with after-school programs, summer camps, community recreation programs, 4-H programs, scout programs, faith-based organizations, and so on.

If individuals from these organizations came to your school for information and advice about reducing bullying in their settings, what assistance could you provide? How might you proactively look to engage these individuals?

You can also raise awareness about the problem of bullying through your local media. The groundwork for a local awareness campaign is already done. The Health Resources and Services Administration's (HRSA) National Bullying Prevention Campaign has developed dynamic, multimedia resources to bring attention to the impact of bullying on young people's lives and "what works" in bullying prevention. Everything you need to create a local media campaign is easily accessible online at www.stopbullyingnow.hrsa.gov.

Here are some other ways that you can also use the local media to promote bullying prevention efforts in the broader community:

- Write an ongoing monthly or bimonthly column in a school or local newspaper to maintain public awareness of the issue of bullying.
- Suggest news stories related to bullying and bullying prevention to your local media, such as stories about school violence or hazing. You might be able to connect bullying to other stories in the news; for example, a crime reporter might be interested in what is being done about bullying after it is revealed that a perpetrator had a personal history of bullying. Work with the reporter to recognize the importance of bullying prevention.
- Write newspaper columns for parents with suggestions on how parents can address bullying at home. Use content from the parent pamphlet (see page 85).

How Do You Identify Key Community Leaders?

Whether your primary goal is to build community support for your program or to distribute anti-bullying messages throughout your community, you will need to identify key community leaders (informal as well as formal) and target groups. One of the best ways to identify community leaders is by involving students. Ideas of how to engage students in these efforts are available on the Teacher Guide CD-ROM.

When Should Your Community Efforts Begin?

Some level of community involvement should begin with your initial implementation phase (for example, including one or two community representatives on your BPCC, or seeking funding or other support for your program). Then it is up to your BPCC to determine an optimal timeline for actively engaging members of your broader community in other bullying prevention efforts.

Some schools focus their initial efforts on schoolwide, classroom, and individual components and explore ways of reaching out to community partners only after their program is functioning fairly smoothly within the school building (in the second and third years of the program, for example). Others reach out to community members and groups immediately, believing that their efforts will be strengthened by community support.

There are a wide variety of ways to involve community members in your bullying prevention efforts. Engaging the community should not be seen as an add-on, but a core component of *OBPP*.

• • •

15

Continuing Your Efforts

WHAT YOU WILL LEARN IN CHAPTER 15	• ways to sustain your *OBPP* efforts over the long term • ways to enhance or expand your *OBPP* efforts

As mentioned earlier, *OBPP* is not a curriculum with a prescribed number of sessions. Instead, it is designed to become a component of the school environment and part of each teacher's classroom routines. In order for the program to be successful, it needs to be continued for more than just a year or two. Research has shown that using the program over the long term continues to reduce bullying and other antisocial behavior.

It is also important to be aware that bullying is a problem that will not be completely eradicated even with your best efforts. Bullying tendencies can arise at any time, and you must be constantly prepared to prevent and actively counter this type of problem. It is therefore necessary to repeat certain components of *OBPP* regularly.

Administrators and members of the BPCC are responsible for ensuring that systematic anti-bullying work continues to be a central theme at the school and that the main principles and components of *OBPP* are followed.

Here are the tasks that need to be completed to continue the program for the long term:

1. **Continue the role of your Bullying Prevention Coordinating Committee and program coordinator.**

   It is important that the BPCC continue to meet for as long as the program is in use. Since this could be an indefinite amount of time, committee members likely will want to rotate on and off the committee or commit to serving two-year terms. Be sure to stagger the rotations of the BPCC so that not all members rotate off at the same time and make sure each new member is trained. It is important to have continuity of ideas.

If the program coordinator position is not a paid position, the person serving as the coordinator may need to rotate as well. Some schools find that having a shared coordinator position (that is, co-coordinators), where a new coordinator steps up every two years, helps reduce the workload and ensures consistent leadership for the group.

2. **Maintain an ongoing relationship with your certified Olweus trainer.**
   It is recommended that during the first year of implementation, schools stay in contact with their certified Olweus trainer at least monthly. After the first year, schools are encouraged to keep in contact with their trainer on a periodic but less frequent basis. You may need to set up a separate contract or agreement with your trainer for this extended consultation, if he or she is not part of your staff.

   Your certified Olweus trainer can help interpret the data from your yearly Olweus Bullying Questionnaire, help organize trainings for new staff, and give presentations to parent groups. This individual could also provide expert help to your school's anti-bullying work, in general, and troubleshoot especially difficult cases of bullying. Updating you on new research findings from the Olweus group of researchers and others is another role the certified Olweus trainer can fulfill.

3. **Hold twice-yearly staff meetings to update staff about *OBPP*.**
   Twice a year (at the beginning of the fall semester and toward the end of the spring semester) all-staff meetings should be organized to review and discuss the core components of your bullying prevention program. These meetings should clarify what is expected of the staff with respect to supervision of students, implementation of the four anti-bullying rules, continuing to conduct class meetings, and procedures for discovering, dealing with, and preventing bullying at school.

   It should be a major objective for all adults at the school to appear as a unified group with the same attitudes against bullying, the same anti-bullying rules, and the same methods for intervening in bullying situations.

The school must bear the marks of a strong "anti-bullying culture" with a distinct adult leadership.

The staff meeting at the beginning of the fall semester should include a summary and assessment of how well *OBPP* has been introduced at the school, which elements have been implemented with fidelity, and which should be strengthened. The spring meeting should first and foremost be a time for summarizing and critically evaluating your school's *OBPP* efforts—which objectives and results have been achieved and which changes or improvements, if any, the school should introduce.

An implementation checklist for ongoing efforts is included on the Schoolwide Guide CD-ROM. Review this checklist once per semester to make sure you are continuing to implement *OBPP* with fidelity. 34

4. **Continue staff discussion groups.**

   After the initial year, we recommend that schools organize at least five staff discussion group meetings per year. The format and structure will be similar to those held during the first year of a school's program. Ideally, the meetings should last for approximately one hour, have a theme that has been announced beforehand, and be well structured. BPCC members (or others who have received the two-day *OBPP* training) should lead these sessions. The composition of these groups could be the same as the earlier staff discussion groups, or you may want to rotate membership somewhat. These groups could also be organized into grade-level teams, if there are no fewer than four and no more than fifteen people on a team.

   The topics of staff discussion groups should be related to bullying and *OBPP* components. At least one of the meetings should be dedicated to refreshing and thoroughly discussing the procedures for dealing with and following up on identified and suspected cases of bullying.

5. **Provide training for new staff.**

   Your school should plan to hold a one-day training for new staff members. To keep expenses low, this training could easily be held for several schools in the vicinity. The purpose of this training is to provide a concentrated introduction to *OBPP,* covering the same topics that were covered in the staff training at the beginning of your program. This training will help new staff members integrate into the existing school culture. Also consider partnering new staff with other staff in a mentoring relationship, so the new staff members feel more supported as they begin to use the program.

6. **Administer the Olweus Bullying Questionnaire on a yearly basis.**
   School personnel should arrange to administer the Olweus Bullying Questionnaire every year to identify successes and areas that still need work. The questionnaire should be administered to all students at the same time (ideally the same week) each year to ensure comparability of students' responses. If your school uses the scannable survey and has Hazelden Publishing process the results, you can purchase a Trends Report for a minimal fee that will show you the differences in results from year to year.

   These new results should be thoroughly evaluated and reported to school staff, parents, and community members on an ongoing basis. The results should also be used for planning your school's ongoing work against bullying.

7. **Evaluate your supervisory system on a regular basis.**
   Your school's supervisory system and plan must be reviewed, assessed critically, and, if necessary, adjusted at least once a year, preferably early in the fall semester. Use feedback from evaluation meetings with staff to update or revise these plans.

8. **Continue to motivate teachers and other staff to actively and consistently enforce the four anti-bullying rules.**
   The four anti-bullying rules are a core component of *OBPP,* and it is important that these rules are firmly in place early in the school year.

RESEARCH FACT

> *OBPP* research has shown that schools with staff members who share the same attitudes toward the use and enforcement of the rules achieve a greater reduction in bullying than other schools.

9. **Continue holding class meetings on a regular basis.**
   Regular class meetings led by the teacher are another important ongoing component of *OBPP.* These class meetings should be used to update and maintain the anti-bullying rules and to keep up the students' commitment and understanding of your school's bullying policies. Teachers should also continue to use role-playing as much as possible. Although bullying will be

a main theme in these class meetings, it is natural that they will gradually focus on other topics related to the students' behavior, well-being, and the school environment as well.

10. Continue to hold an annual student kick-off event.

It is recommended that you hold an *OBPP* student kick-off event at the beginning of each new school year. Use this event as an opportunity to celebrate your success and to remind students of the anti-bullying rules and consequences and their own roles in creating a more positive school environment. Consider a new theme each year for this event.

11. Continue to keep parents well informed about the program.

Continue to keep parents well informed about your school's bullying prevention and intervention efforts through schoolwide parent meetings, through class-level parent meetings, or during individual parent conferences. Also continue to have parents serving on your BPCC.

The beginning of each school year is a natural time to give parents updated information about *OBPP* and to invite them to participate in school parent meetings. Results of the yearly Olweus Bullying Questionnaire can be shared at these meetings.

Teachers should also contact parents early in the beginning of each school year to establish positive rapport and to go over the procedures that will be used if bullying occurs. Teachers can let parents know that they should contact the school if their child reports bullying or any other problematic behavior. All parents should be regularly assured that steps will be taken to address the bullying.

12. Other ideas to consider.

During the first year of implementation, you will need to spend a lot of time integrating the core components of *OBPP* into your school's practices. After the first year, you may have time to begin to look at other issues related to bullying or to consider expanding your anti-bullying efforts. For information on innovative ideas other schools have used, see the Schoolwide Guide CD-ROM. 35

Such topics to be addressed could include the following:

- Are there ways to strengthen processes and procedures to make your bullying prevention efforts even more effective?

- How will you deal with crisis situations that involve bullying?
- How do your bullying efforts fit with other state and federal mandates? How can you report your bullying efforts in compliance with these mandates?
- How can your experiences and the knowledge you have gained from using the program be better shared with others in your school and community?

In order to maintain a focus on bullying prevention, your BPCC should consider ways to enhance the program, such as

- networking with other schools that are also using the program in your area to share successes, challenges, and ideas for the future. Your certified Olweus trainer can help you establish this network.
- holding discussions or meetings with coordinators and/or committee members from other schools.
- sending out press releases and announcements about your school's progress and success.
- locating other supplemental prevention programs that complement *OBPP.* Contact Hazelden Publishing for more information at 1-800-328-9000 or 1-651-213-4000 or www.hazelden.org/olweus.

Funding

To sustain your program, you may also wish to secure more funding (although the cost of the program in years two and beyond is much less than the start-up costs for year one). Look for grant money or funding sources in your community. You could also look on the *OBPP* Web site at www.clemson.org/olweus or the Hazelden Publishing Web site at www.hazelden.org/olweus. These Web sites may periodically have announcements or information about funding sources.

There is also grant information available on the Schoolwide Guide CD-ROM (see page 12). Additional ideas for extending the program in your school's classrooms are provided in the Teacher Guide, chapter 10.

Your long-term commitment to *OBPP* will bring many rewards, as the program becomes more and more central to how your school functions and how staff and students behave toward one another. This commitment on the part of all school staff will have a tremendous impact on the lives of your students, both now and in the future.

• • •

16

Evaluating the Impact of Your Program

WHAT YOU WILL LEARN IN CHAPTER 16	
	• ways to use the Olweus Bullying Questionnaire to evaluate your program over the long-term • about other tools that can be used to provide evaluation data

It is important to continue to evaluate the *Olweus Bullying Prevention Program* at your school in order to understand whether the program is being implemented as it was intended (that is, with fidelity), how adult attitudes and responses are changing, and how bullying and other antisocial behaviors among students are changing. Program evaluations that focus on program outcomes and on the process of implementation will be the most informative.

When Should You Begin Evaluating Your Program?

Evaluation of your program should begin the first year and should continue over time.

As was mentioned earlier, for students in grades 4–7, most of the positive results have been obtained already after eight months of intervention work, given reasonably good implementation of the program. For students in grades 8–10, it may take somewhat more time, maybe two years, to achieve equally good results. Both the school staff and parents need to understand that this program does not offer temporary quick fixes, but rather long-term solutions that will endure.

Students who bully others need to repeatedly experience that their behavior will not be accepted and there will always be consequences. Most changes in the school climate will not come in a week or two, but after continued effort on the part of the staff and students.

What Kinds of Evaluation Should Be Done?

Measuring Program Outcomes

The Olweus Bullying Questionnaire is the primary tool recommended to measure outcomes of *OBPP*. This questionnaire is administered at the same time each year with all students (grades 3 and up) in the school. It provides one important quantitative measure of the effectiveness of your *OBPP* efforts and will help you to identify areas of progress and need.

This student perspective will help you to know whether targeted areas and behaviors have been influenced by the program and whether new ones have emerged. The data will help you make sure your supervisory system is working and that students are being positively affected by the program.

When using the questionnaire to examine changes in students' responses over time, it is important to consider three issues.

First, as mentioned in chapter 5, you should expect to see changes in some but not all of students' responses. For example, with time, it is reasonable to expect changes in the prevalence of bullying and in students' perceptions of teachers' responsiveness to bullying. On the other hand, it is unlikely that you will see changes in students' reports of which forms of bullying are the most frequent (verbal bullying generally remains the most common form of bullying) or in the grade and gender of students who bully (students are most often bullied by students in the same grade or a higher grade; boys are usually bullied by boys, while girls are bullied by boys and girls).

Second, judging your school's success simply on the short-term results from the Olweus Bullying Questionnaire may be misleading. Because *OBPP* efforts teach students and adults to recognize bullying and encourage them to report it, the questionnaire may actually show an increase in bullying reports after the first year—behaviors that have been previously hidden or underreported are now brought to light. This does not necessarily mean that there has been an increase in bullying behavior; rather, it may reflect an increased awareness of and self-reporting on the questionnaire.

Finally, when comparing data from one year to the next, it is important to take age-related changes in bullying problems into account. To do this, you should compare students of the same age/grade. For example, compare the data for fifth-graders in one year with fifth-graders in the next year. This is because there is a natural developmental change in bullying as students get older (for example, the number of students who are bullied usually decreases as students get older).

Other Evaluation Measures

There are other ways to evaluate the effects of the program in addition to assessing changes in bullying behavior and attitudes through the Olweus Bullying Questionnaire. Some schools have used other outcome measures to supplement their evaluation. Here are some other types of data that may be beneficial to look at:

- Absentee and/or truancy rates might provide information on how students feel about being at school.
- Student test scores might indicate whether the learning environment has improved.
- Discipline reports might indicate decreases in aggressive or disruptive behavior.
- Discipline reports from bus routes might indicate how the program is spilling over into areas outside of the school.
- The numbers of suspensions might indicate how consequences are carried out or how the number of suspensions may have changed since the program was implemented.
- Critical incident rates in school might indicate whether problems such as student fights and vandalism have been reduced.
- Other surveys that have questions referring to school climate may indicate the effectiveness of your bullying prevention program in affecting the climate of the classroom or school.

If these variables (absentee rates, discipline reports, and so on) are used to evaluate your program, be sure to obtain data before the program is implemented as well as after the program has begun (and at regular intervals thereafter).

Because adults in your school play a large part in *OBPP* implementation and success, it may be very helpful to assess changes in their attitudes and behaviors with regard to preventing and addressing bullying. Some schools have administered questionnaires to teachers, parents, and playground supervisors at the same time that they survey students each year.

Staff Process Evaluations

A process evaluation assesses the "delivery" of *OBPP* by describing and documenting how well the program is being implemented. This type of evaluation should include a focus on fidelity—how closely the program is being implemented compared to the model.

Examples of process evaluations include

- regularly using the Implementation Checklists (see page 97) to measure how closely staff have implemented the program to the intended model
- surveying teachers on key components of the Implementation Checklists, such as: Did you hold class meetings once a week? Did you use role-playing on a regular basis in your classroom?
- administering a take-home parent evaluation that assesses parents' perceptions of the program and their involvement in it
- passing out 3x5-inch note cards at the first and last staff meeting each year and asking staff to list one or two positive changes they have noticed in students, themselves, or the school climate as a result of *OBPP*
- holding focus groups with parents, staff, and/or students (separately) to get their input into the program and areas for improvement

As part of your process evaluation, maintain a portfolio of critical program information, such as

- Maintain a log of minutes of your BPCC meetings (you can store these electronically or in a notebook).
- Use your BPCC workbook (see page 31) to guide your efforts and set goals each year. Keep copies of it to track ways that your school efforts have evolved over time. You can use this to note changes in your school's supervision plan as well as special events.
- Establish record-keeping tools for teachers to complete whenever they conduct a class meeting. A Class Meeting Activity Log is provided on the Teacher Guide CD-ROM. Collect copies of these logs and keep them in a central place for periodic review by BPCC members.

  These logs will give you a sense of not only who is doing class meetings and how often, but the topics being covered and areas where teachers may need help so that you can improve teacher commitment and strengthen skills.
- Keep similar records of staff discussion groups and periodically review these to highlight staff development needs.
- Keep track of where your anti-bullying rules posters have been placed each year; also keep copies of student handbooks or other school handbooks that include anti-bullying policies and procedures.

- Keep agendas of staff and parent training events and indicate the numbers in attendance.
- Take pictures at kick-off events, of students participating in class meetings, or at other special events. Keep a scrapbook of pictures and samples of student work related to bullying.
- Keep copies of your graduated discipline plan and positive and negative consequences.
- Review class meeting logs to determine consistency and issues that need to be addressed.

Who Should Be Informed about the Results?

One way of keeping bullying prevention a main focus in your school is to report any evaluation results to the entire school community, including staff, students, and parents. It is also important to communicate the results to your district administration to maintain their continued support of the program.

Your community contacts, funders, and other connections will also want to know how the program is going and how you will continue to meet the needs of students, as indicated by the results of your evaluation. Press releases in local newspapers can help spread the word about the progress of the program as well.

It is strongly recommended that the results of any evaluation and/or of the questionnaire be communicated to others in terms of overall outcomes, rather than focusing in on specific grades.

In most school districts, Olweus Bullying Questionnaire data are considered "public information" under the Freedom of Information Act. While you will want to share results with parents and the community, it is important to present the results in a way that protects student and teacher privacy and to provide information in a context that ensures it will be appropriately interpreted and understood.

How Can We Afford to Evaluate the Program?

Although evaluating the program does cost money, it is important to do evaluations, especially if you are looking to seek additional outside funding to keep your program going. Most funding agencies will want to see evaluation data before they offer a second round of funding.

The cost of evaluating the program should be included when planning your program budget. If you do not have sufficient money or staff time to evaluate the program as thoroughly as you would like, consider partnering with a local university or college, as there may be students or faculty members who could assist you. Often college students are in need of experience in program evaluation as part of their course work.

Evaluating the program will help you understand how *OBPP* has affected your school and students, and what further action is required to help your school continue to reduce bullying behavior.

• • •

17

Implementing the Program in High School

WHAT YOU WILL LEARN IN CHAPTER 17	• ways to adapt the program for use in a high school setting • brief description of additional issues to address at the high school level

The *Olweus Bullying Prevention Program* is designed for use in grades 1–9, and all research studies on the program's effectiveness have looked at students in grades 4–9. Although there has been great interest in providing *OBPP* at the high school level, no formal program has been developed for those grade levels yet, nor have evaluations been done on programs adapted to this older audience.

That said, some schools are piloting the program in high schools now, particularly in districts where they have successfully implemented *OBPP* at the elementary and middle school level. It is not recommended that a school district start with high school.

With this in mind, there are some things schools may want to look at in terms of adaptations if they would like to provide *OBPP* to high school students. They are as follows:

- Closely monitor student behavior. The challenge at the high school level is to develop a system to monitor student behavior. It can be particularly challenging to do this in a high school environment. The school's BPCC must really look at monitoring as an important part of the program.
- Address not only the basic definition of bullying, but also related behaviors that may emerge (or be more common) among this age group, such as sexual harassment, dating violence, homophobic behavior, and gang-related violence.

- Identify curriculum resources, student literature, audiovisual materials, student plays, and other materials that could help generate discussions or activities that are developmentally appropriate for older students.
- Be clear that policies and procedures against bullying do not replace laws and policies that are in place to address sexual harassment, disability harassment, racial harassment, hazing, and other illegal behaviors. All school districts have policies that prohibit harassment of students based on race, color, national origin, sex, and disability, because federal law requires them to do so if they are to receive federal funds.
- Encourage students to take leadership roles in guiding class meeting discussions.
- Train high school students to present basic bullying concepts to younger students, through being part of a school's kick-off event, presenting skits in classrooms, or serving as aides in conducting class meetings. Many high schools now have community service or involvement requirements for graduation.
- Challenge students to do class- or team-level projects that will promote an anti-bullying message in the community. Ideas for student involvement with community projects are provided on the Teacher Guide CD-ROM.
- Carefully consider whether or not to hold a kick-off event, as older students may react negatively to such events and/or perceive them to be juvenile. Ensure that you have ample student input into the planning of any event designed to launch your program.
- Have students create posters that provide a more high school–oriented message about bullying and the four anti-bullying rules. Hang these posters around the school.
- Have students serve on your BPCC and play an active role in the development of the program. Consider having a representative from each grade level on the committee or create an all-student advisory committee.
- Ask student representatives to help you "redesign" your school's public spaces or schedule to reduce or prevent bullying. Use their experience and knowledge of school issues to address this new redesign.
- Schools often have social action committees and clubs (such as violence prevention groups, gay-straight alliances, and groups designed to promote racial understanding and harmony, among others). Utilize these resources and/or organize a student "club" whose focus is on a positive school climate,

inclusion, or harmony among students, and whose membership is open to all students.

Although this is a brief overview of what could be done to adapt the program for high school students, it hopefully provides some ideas of ways to implement the program with this older audience.

• • •

Notes

Introduction

1. Dan Olweus, *Bullying at School: What We Know and What We Can Do* (Oxford, England: Blackwell Publishing, 1993).

2. James Alan Fox, Delbert S. Elliott, R. Gil Kerlikowske, Sanford A. Newman, and William Christeson, *Bullying Prevention Is Crime Prevention,* a report by Fight Crime: Invest in Kids, 2003. Available at www.fightcrime.org.

Chapter 1: Introducing the *Olweus Bullying Prevention Program*

1. Dan Olweus, "Bully/Victim Problems among Schoolchildren: Basic Facts and Effects of a School-based Intervention Program," in *The Development and Treatment of Childhood Aggression*, ed. D. Pepler and K. Rubin (Hillsdale, N.J.: Erlbaum, 1991), 411–48; Dan Olweus, "A Useful Evaluation Design, and Effects of the Olweus Bullying Prevention Program," *Psychology, Crime & Law* 11 (2005): 389–402; Dan Olweus and S. Limber, *Blueprints for Violence Prevention: Bullying Prevention Program* (Boulder: Institute of Behavioral Science, University of Colorado, 1999); Jan Helge Kallestad and Dan Olweus, "Predicting Teachers' and Schools' Implementation of the Olweus Bullying Prevention Program: A Multilevel Study," *Prevention and Treatment* 6 (October 2003): 3–21. Available at www.journals.apa.org/prevention/volume6/pre0060021a.html.

2. Kallestad and Olweus, "Predicting Teachers' and Schools' Implementation of the Olweus Bullying Prevention Program."

3. C. B. Fleming, K. P. Haggerty, R. F. Catalano, T. W. Harachi, J. J. Mazza, and D. H. Gruman, "Do Social and Behavioral Characteristics Targeted by Preventive Interventions Predict Standardized Test Scores and Grades?" *Journal of School Health* 75 (2005): 342–49.

4. Olweus, "Bully/Victim Problems among Schoolchildren."

5. Dan Olweus, "Vad Skapar Aggressiva Barn?" [What Creates Aggressive Children?] in *Normkrise og Oppdragelse* [Norm Crisis and Child Rearing], ed. A. O. Telhaug and S. E. Vestre (Oslo, Norway: Didakta, 1981); Dan Olweus, "Sweden," in *The Nature of School Bullying: A Cross-National Perspective,* ed. P. K. Smith, Y. Morita, J. Junger-Tas, D. Olweus, R. Catalano, and P. Slee (London: Routledge, 1999), 7–27.

Chapter 3: Getting Started in Your School

1. Dan Olweus, *Bullying at School: What We Know and What We Can Do* (Oxford, England: Blackwell Publishing, 1993); J. Juvonen, S. Graham, and M. A. Schuster, "Bullying among Young Adolescents: The Strong, the Weak, and the Troubled," *Pediatrics* 112 (2003): 1231–37; R. J. Baumeister, J. D. Campbell, J. I. Krueger, and K. D. Vohs, "Does Self-Esteem Cause Better Performance, Interpersonal Success, Happiness, or Healthier Lifestyles?" *Psychological Science in the Public Interest* 4 (2003): 1–44.

Chapter 8: Introducing School Bullying Rules and Consequences

1. S. P. Limber, "Addressing Youth Bullying Behaviors," in *Educational Forum on Adolescent Health: Youth Bullying*, ed. M. Fleming and K. Towey (Chicago: American Medical Association, 2002), 5–16.

Chapter 9: Refining Your School's Supervisory System

1. Dan Olweus, *Bullying at School: What We Know and What We Can Do* (Oxford, England: Blackwell Publishing, 1993), 25.

Chapter 12: Supporting the Program in the Classroom

1. Dan Olweus and F. D. Alsaker, "Assessing Change in a Cohort Longitudinal Study with Hierarchical Data," in *Problems and Methods in Longitudinal Research*, ed. D. Magnusson, L. R. Bergman, G. Rudinger, and B. Törestad (New York: Cambridge University Press, 1991), 107–32.

• • •

About the Authors

Dan Olweus, Ph.D.

For more than thirty-five years, Dr. Dan Olweus, research professor of psychology, affiliated with the Research Center for Health Promotion (HEMIL) at the University of Bergen in Norway, has been involved in research and intervention work in the area of bullying problems among schoolchildren and youth. In 1970, he started a large-scale project that is now generally regarded as the first scientific study of bullying problems in the world, published as a book in Scandinavia in 1973 and in 1978 in the United States under the title *Aggression in the Schools: Bullies and Whipping Boys.*

In the 1980s, Dr. Olweus conducted the first systematic intervention study against bullying in the world, which documented a number of quite positive effects of what is now the *Olweus Bullying Prevention Program (OBPP).* He was also the first to study the problem of bullying of students by teachers. Since 2001, he has been the leader of a government-initiated national initiative implementing *OBPP* on a large-scale basis in Norwegian elementary and junior high schools.

Dr. Olweus is generally recognized as a pioneer and founding father of research on bullying problems and as a world-leading expert in this area both by the research community and by society at large. His book *Bullying at School: What We Know and What We Can Do* has been translated into fifteen different languages. Dr. Olweus has received a number of awards and recognitions for his research and intervention work, including the "Distinguished Contributions to Public Policy for Children" award by the Society for Research in Child Development (SRCD). He has been a fellow at the Center for Advanced Study in the Behavioral Sciences (CASBS) in Stanford, California.

Susan P. Limber, Ph.D., MLS

Susan P. Limber is director of the Center on Youth Participation and Human Rights and professor of psychology at Clemson University. She is a developmental psychologist who received her masters and doctoral degrees in psychology at the University of Nebraska–Lincoln. She also holds a Masters of Legal Studies from Nebraska.

Dr. Limber's research and writing have focused on legal and psychological issues related to youth violence (particularly bullying among children), child protection, and children's rights. She directed the first wide-scale implementation and evaluation of the *Olweus Bullying Prevention Program* in the United States and co-authored the *Blueprint for the Bullying Prevention Program* as well as many other articles on the topic of bullying. In recent years, she has directed the training for the *Olweus Bullying Prevention Program* in the United States. She has provided consultation to the National Bullying Prevention Campaign, supported by the Health Resources and Services Administration.

In 1997, she received the Saleem Shah Award for early career excellence in psychology-law policy, awarded by the American Psychology-Law Society of the American Psychological Association (Division 41) and the American Academy of Forensic Psychiatry. In 2004, Dr. Limber received the American Psychological Association's Early Career Award for Psychology in the Public Interest.

Vicki Crocker Flerx, Ph.D.

Vicki C. Flerx is an *Olweus Bullying Prevention Program* training director and a research assistant professor at the University of South Carolina's Institute for Families in Society. She has expertise in both public and mental health. Prior to earning her doctorate in public health, Dr. Flerx spent fifteen years as a therapist working in psychiatric settings and focusing on women and youth who were victims of abuse. Dr. Flerx was one of the University of South Carolina researchers who first brought the *Olweus Bullying Prevention Program* to the United States. Dr. Flerx trains and consults nationally to support the dissemination of the program. In addition, she has conducted research in family violence, including intimate partner violence, child abuse, and children exposed to domestic violence.

Nancy Mullin, M.Ed.

Nancy Mullin is an *Olweus Bullying Prevention Program* training director and a research scientist at the Wellesley Centers for Women at Wellesley College, where she is director of both the Project on Teasing and Bullying and the Preschool Empathy Project. Ms. Mullin is a nationally known trainer and consultant in the area of bullying prevention and developing awareness about the negative effects that bullying and related gender-role stereotypes have on both school climate and student performance. She has been involved in research, curriculum development, and training. She also coordinated the Massachusetts Bullying Prevention Project, the first statewide *Olweus Bullying Prevention Program* school initiative in the United States. Ms. Mullin is the author of several publications about bullying, including *Quit It! A Teacher's Guide on Teasing and Bullying for Use with Students in Grades K–3*, a recommended *OBPP* supplemental resource.

Jane Riese, L.S.W.

Jane Riese is an *Olweus Bullying Prevention Program* training director as well as the director of Bullying Prevention Services at Family-Child Resources, Inc. in York, Pennsylvania. A social worker and prevention educator since 1982, Ms. Riese helped to pilot the early Olweus trainers certification process and assisted with coordination of the first U.S. Olweus Training of Trainers held in 2001 in Pennsylvania. She currently oversees *Olweus Bullying Prevention Program* implementation in numerous schools throughout the country. Ms. Riese created and directed dialogue-based restorative justice programming in her community and was also the director of a prosecution-based victim-witness office. She has served on the board of directors of the international Victim Offender Mediation Association since 2000.

Marlene Snyder, Ph.D.

Marlene Snyder is an associate professor at the Institute of Family and Neighborhood Life, Clemson University, in South Carolina and serves as the *Olweus Bullying Prevention Program's* national point of contact. She can be contacted at nobully@clemson.edu or 1-864-710-4562.

Dr. Snyder is also a training director for the *Olweus Bullying Prevention Program.* She has served as a national and international conference speaker, trainer, and technical assistance consultant for educational, mental health, child welfare, and juvenile justice agencies, as well as parent education organizations. Dr. Snyder consults regularly with a wide variety of professional and community organizations on a range of topics related to bullying prevention and intervention. She has also written extensively on the topic of ADHD, including a book entitled *ADHD & Driving: A Guide for Parents of Teens with ADHD*. Dr. Snyder is the founding president of the International Bullying Prevention Association.

• • •

Hazelden Foundation, a national nonprofit organization founded in 1949, helps people reclaim their lives from the disease of addiction. With nearly 60 years of knowledge and experience, Hazelden's comprehensive approach to addiction addresses the full range of individual, family, and professional needs, including addiction treatment and continuing care services for youth and adults, publishing, research, higher learning, public education, and advocacy.

A life of recovery is lived "one day at a time." Hazelden publications, both educational and inspirational, support and strengthen lifelong recovery. In 1954, Hazelden published *Twenty-Four Hours a Day,* the first daily meditation book for recovering alcoholics, and Hazelden continues to publish works to inspire and guide individuals in treatment and recovery, and their loved ones. Professionals who work to prevent and treat addiction also turn to Hazelden for evidence-based curricula, informational materials, and videos for use in schools, treatment programs, and correctional programs.

Through published works, Hazelden extends the reach of hope, encouragement, help, and support to individuals, families, and communities affected by addiction and related issues.

For questions about Hazelden publications, please call 800-328-9000 or visit us online at hazelden.org/bookstore.